PAKISTAN ON THE GLOBE

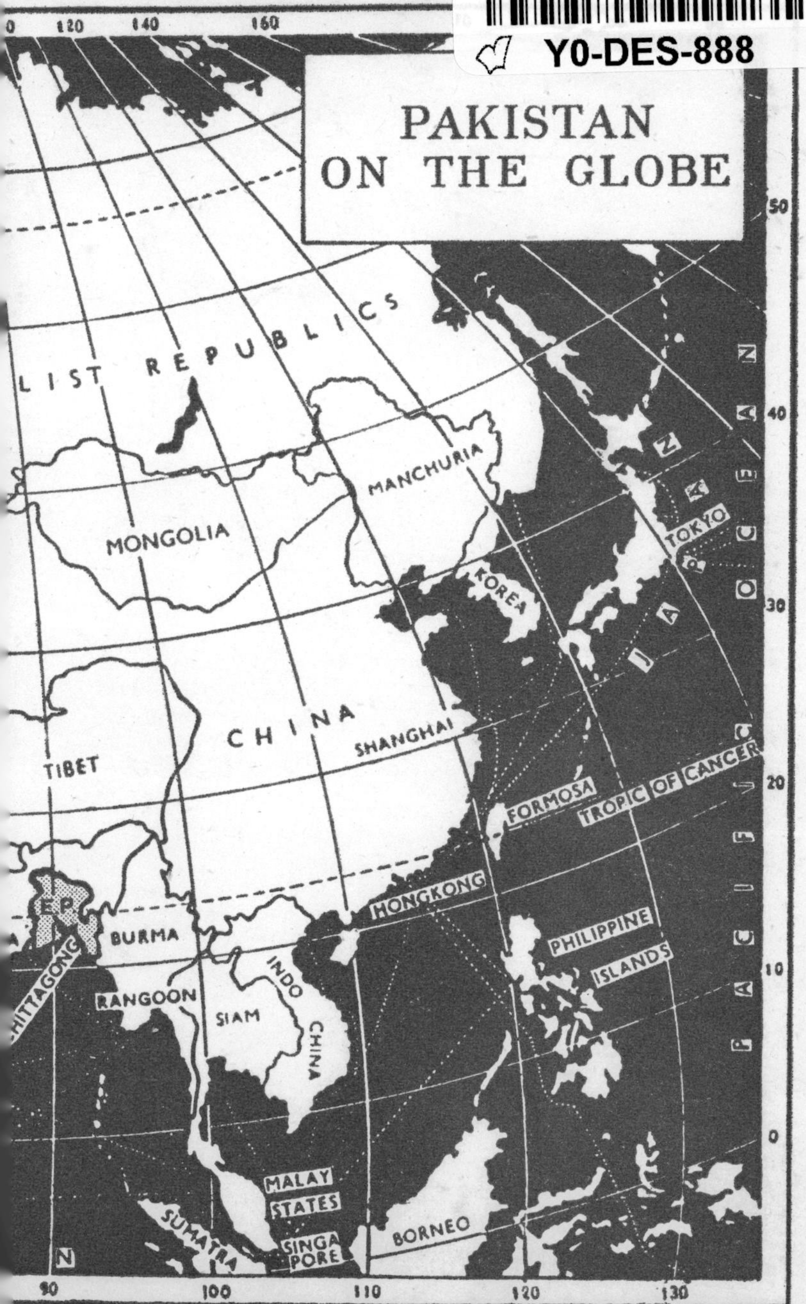

YOUNG PAKISTAN

To Dr. Hamidullah

With sincere compliments from the author

Major Mohammad Khan

1st July 1951

YOUNG PAKISTAN

A CITIZENSHIP READER
FOR SECONDARY SCHOOLS AND
ADULT INSTITUTIONS

by
RAFIQ M. KHAN
B.A. Honours
(National Muslim University, Aligarh)
Administrative Officer, Information Department
Pakistan's Mission in the U.K.

and

HERBERT S. STARK
B.A. Honours (Oxon)
Oxford Diploma in Education

GEOFFREY CUMBERLEGE
OXFORD UNIVERSITY PRESS
London   New York   Toronto
1951

Oxford University Press, Amen House, London E.C.4
GLASGOW NEW YORK TORONTO MELBOURNE WELLINGTON
BOMBAY CALCUTTA MADRAS CAPE TOWN
Geoffrey Cumberlege, Publisher to the University

Printed in Great Britain

AUTHORS' PREFACE

In presenting this book to the educational world of Pakistan, the authors desire to make it clear that they have written these chapters in their private capacity, and that in no particular should their facts or opinions be taken as reflecting the official policy or attitude of the Pakistan Government or the Government of the United Kingdom.

At the same time, all possible care has been taken to verify each fact and to offer as accurate a picture as is humanly possible.

R. M. KHAN
H. S. STARK

LONDON
1 *January* 1951

FOREWORD

by ALLAMA ABDULLA YUSUF ALI,
I.C.S. (retd.), Fellow of the Royal Society of Arts, Fellow of the Royal Society of Literature, and Fellow of the Royal Institute of International Affairs.

PAKISTAN'S older boys and girls, and their parents and teachers, will hail this book with real delight. Although it is intended as a text-book, it is something far better than that; it is an epic in prose, telling them and the world of one of the greatest wonders of the present age—the creation of a most promising young State. It goes even beyond that, for it succeeds in stimulating their patriotic pride at the marvellous achievements which have been crowded into the first few critical years of Pakistan's existence.

This thrilling story shows how the most appalling difficulties, which beset the Partition of 1947, are being conquered by the loyal determination of the people and the wise leadership of their Government. The book sets out in detail what has been accomplished in every field of national endeavour—in Defence, Industry, Agriculture, Co-operation, Irrigation, Health, Education, Transport, and Communications; the development of cities, the promotion of culture, the uplift of women, and the sealing of our national unity in the light of the Islamic way of life.

Not satisfied with that, the authors have given a full picture of the ideals and methods of democracy. They have amply explained also Pakistan's relations with the British Commonwealth of Nations, of which it is a member, and with our immediate neighbours. The important 'World Peace' function of the United Nations Organization is explained in clear and simple language, so that any young person can understand why Pakistan itself supports that Organization.

Moreover, the book has been written in pleasant and simple language throughout. Although a wealth of facts is supplied, there is nothing that is beyond the comprehension of the average boy or girl aged between 15 and 19. One of the authors is a highly qualified teacher, and the other a research scholar; both the writers are deeply experienced publicists. They have not attempted to pump barren knowledge into the minds of the younger generation, but have skilfully adopted the method of proceeding 'from the known to the unknown'. Their aim has been to set young minds thinking, to help their readers to link up vital facts, and explain natural tendencies in the development of national consciousness. I sincerely believe they have succeeded to a degree which has been attained in no other book yet written about our country. There is, in fact, so far as I am aware, no other book about Pakistan expressly written for our younger generation.

A country is as great only as its people. True greatness is derived, not from the material wealth surrounding them, but from their ability to unite, to see the good in each other, and to pursue the path of nation-building with courage and the spirit of trust and co-operation—above all, to use their natural gift of thoughtfulness.

I commend *Young Pakistan* because I believe it will exercise a most beneficial influence on our young men and women, who will be the nation of to-morrow.

NATIONAL LIBERAL CLUB
LONDON, S.W.1
18 *November* 1950

CONTENTS

PREFACE *page* v

FOREWORD *page* vii

I A SACRED TRUST

How Pakistan became independent—the 'Two Nation' theory—the story of the Indian Reforms—Muslims' later fears—Hindus' efforts to gain supremacy—Anti-Muslim campaign—Muslim League's victory—the 1947 Partition—an Islamic State achieved—the 'Objectives Resolution'—Provisional Government—on the road to prosperity. *page* 1

II FIVE THOUSAND YEARS OF HISTORY

Early civilization—many relics found—Mohenjo-daro and Harappa—their ancient inhabitants—Aryan invasion—later invaders—Moghals and British. *page* 9

III THE TWO PAKISTANS ARE ONE

Eastern Bengal's early history—rise of Dacca—Shaista Khan's successes—Dacca's decline—the 1905 Partition of Bengal—Muslim rejoicings—Dacca's revival—geographical similarities. *page* 17

IV OUR PEOPLE AND THEIR CUSTOMS

Racial origin—now common bonds—religious link—toleration and protection of other religions—population figures—distribution of communities—the races of Eastern Bengal—mainly agricultural—comparison with other countries. *page* 22

V WHAT SELF-GOVERNMENT MEANS

Historical outline of systems of government—election explained by analogy—development of 'Parliament'—law-making process—'Administration' and its functions—the chief departments—justice and the interpretation of the laws—'local bodies' and *panchayats*—the franchise—'Democracy' defined. *page* 30

VI   AN ASSEMBLY AT WORK

The 'constituencies'—'Elections' and the machinery of 'polling'—an Assembly meeting—the 'Party System'—'Legislative process' in detail—'Money Bills'—difference between Central and Provincial Governments.
page 38

VII   OUR DEFENCE FORCES

The value of our freedom and possessions—our love of peace—but we must be ready to guard against attack—so we have defence forces on a scientific basis—all volunteers—Defence Ministry—difficulties overcome—the Army and its personnel—Navy's functions and strength—naval bases and training—the Pakistan Air Force, its personnel, bases, and training.
page 46

VIII   THE FACTORS OF PRODUCTION

'Land', 'Labour', and 'Capital'—the 'wealth' in and under our soil—geographical aspects—abundant and intelligent workers in need of better methods and training in agriculture—training of industrial labour—marketing of products—capital and its functions—the need of thrift—co-ordination of land, labour, and capital—opportunities for young Pakistanis to pull their weight.
page 56

IX   LIFE IN OUR VILLAGES

Agriculture is and will long remain our chief occupation—a nation of village-dwellers—conservative outlook—housing in East and West Pakistan—community spirit—self-contained units—still too dependent on natural conditions—need to learn more occupations—health conditions cause much concern—importance of educating the rural masses—scope for improving rural economy and social level—how rural life has progressed in other lands.
page 62

X   WATER MEANS WEALTH

The great difference between East and West as regards water for crops—extent of cultivation—historical changes in climate of West Pakistan—wells, 'inundation' canals, and 'perennial' canals—Moghals laid foundations of canal system—British developed canals into biggest network in world—figures showing past and

CONTENTS xiii

future irrigation projects in West Pakistan—drainage need in East Pakistan—schemes to clear *khals* and rivers—great scope and prospects. *page* 70

XI THE SOIL AND ITS PROTECTION

Contents of alluvial soil—how plants live and derive nourishment—importance of water—past neglect of the soil—why deserts spread—erosion and denudation—how to check and reconquer deserts—need to 'return' organic matter to the soil—value of manure—soil research. *page* 78

XII OUR CROPS AND OUR LIVESTOCK

Difference between 'food crops' and 'money crops'—value of animals and birds—foods for livestock—improvement of breeds—chief food crops (rice, wheat, etc.)—nature of 'money crops'—jute and its cultivation—cotton cultivation and value of long staple—tea and its production—timber and its uses—tobacco and oilseeds. *page* 85

XIII OUR INDUSTRIES

Only still in early stages—we are mainly producers of 'raw materials'—but we want to make more goods for ourselves—1947 handicaps and lack of factories—labour available—Government encouragement to private enterprise and capital investments—training of technicians—committees investigate the possibilities of development—need of providing 'power'—fuel and mineral resources—building up of steel industry—setting up of jute and cotton mills—fostering of woollen industry—growth of cottage industries—'Buy Pakistani Products'. *page* 94

XIV CO-OPERATIVE SOCIETIES

The basic idea explained—simple 'Co-operative Consumers' Society'—benefits of marketing societies—co-operative banks—agricultural societies—co-operative housing—a special Government department looks after co-operation—why the *baniya* used to flourish—now replaced by co-operative credit—avoidance of 'middlemen'—world-wide spread—great co-operative system in Britain. *page* 103

XV Transport and Communications

Man's inventiveness—Pakistan's system already developed in 1947—the railways of East and West, their routes and functions—need for development and efficient standard—roads, their nature and extent—need for rubber-tired vehicles—river and canal navigation—civil aviation, vital links—posts, telegraphs, and radio network.

page 113

XVI Cities, Ports, and Towns

Man's social instincts—historical outline—bad planning of old towns—to-day we have better ideas—reasons for ill-health and congestion—functions and growth of municipalities—civic sense—Karachi's history—influx of refugees into Karachi—'Greater Karachi' plan—Chittagong's history and importance—development plans—'Chalna' port project—Dacca's improvement.

page 123

XVII Life at School and College

Why we receive education—in primitive days—expansion of knowledge—invention of language—illiteracy still widespread in Pakistan—plans to stamp out ignorance among the masses—a profitable 'investment'—religious motive—the threefold aims of education—promotion of secondary education—higher education necessary—State scholarships—adult education. *page* 133

XVIII Health and Strength

Good physique of nation—but scourge of epidemics—dirt and hunger as the chief enemies of man—importance of fuller and better diet for the masses—'Prevention is better than cure'—still widespread ignorance of sanitation—how we can help to fight epidemics—'curing of ailments'—lack of hospitals and nurses in 1947—now making up the shortages—need of more women doctors—medical research—anti-malaria and anti-T.B. campaigns—health laws—cleanliness first—'Healthy mind in a healthy body' is also true of nations. *page* 143

XIX Sport and Good Sportsmanship

Keen interest of populace—natural inclination—physical and mental benefit—moral character developed—teaches respect for law and order—'Playing the Game'—co-operative spirit trained—

liking for Western sport—good international record—household names—our Olympic Association—future developments—British and American examples—how all can help—the Quaid-i-Azam's inspiring advice. *page* 152

XX Women of Pakistan

Mr. Jinnah's message—women have set a great example—entry into public life—'the better half' of the nation—great scope for talents—various occupations—founding of All-Pakistan Women's Association—help to refugees—need of doctors, nurses, and teachers—women's industries—beautiful products—Girl Guides—Women's National Guards—true patriots. *page* 162

XXI In the Service of the Public

The will of the people—how it is expressed—delegation of that will to the Assemblies and the Ministries—civil servants are the machinery—education and training—honesty and fairness—anti-corruption law—promotion prospects—methods of recruitment—list of departments—the committee system as a democratic device—non-official share in planning of development and national life. *page* 171

XXII Our Cultural Heritage

Culture defined; its primitive origins—discovery of music and art—gradual refinement of tastes—differences due to natural influences—effect of invasions—1,000 years of Islamic contact and descent—distinct and separate from Hindu culture—Persian influence predominates—architectural example—printing and the fine arts—Urdu poetry—continuation of contact with Islamic lands—modern literary trends. *page* 180

XXIII Pakistan's Place in the British Commonwealth

Spirit of equal partnership and mutual help—the Commonwealth units—different from old 'British Empire'—short sketch of Empire's growth—the colonies—no artificial ties—all dominions equally free and sovereign countries—systems of joint consultation—common status as 'British subjects' is due to common allegiance to the Crown—area and population table—why Pakistan is of interest to the Commonwealth—Imperial Preference and other benefits. *page* 188

CONTENTS

XXIV Our Nearest Neighbours

Tour of frontiers of West Pakistan and East Pakistan—our friendship with Persia—cultural and other links with Persia—Persia's progress resembles ours—Afghanistan's disappointing attitude—Afghans still backward—Kashmir's history and present problem—need of better understanding with Bharat—trade and friendship with Burma—our contacts with Russia and China. *page* 197

XXV The United Nations Organization

We dread war—war as a destroyer in 1918 and 1939—causes of the two World Wars—failure of the League of Nations—still danger of conflict due to different ideologies—UNO formed by peace-loving nations—Charter of the United Nations and the objects of UNO—the General Assembly—the Security Council—UNO's special councils—UNESCO, WHO, etc., and Pakistan's participation—world brotherhood supported by Islam. *page* 207

XXVI The Makers of Pakistan

Gratitude to our founders—the Quaid-i-Azam's career and services—Hazrat Sayed Jamaluddin Afghani's Pan-Islamic revival—Sir Syed Ahmed Khan's efforts to restore Muslim prosperity in India—Aligarh achievement—Syed Amir Ali's support of Muslim social and educational reforms—Allama Mohammed Iqbal's conception of a separate Muslim State of Pakistan. *page* 217

EPILOGUE   *page* 227

APPENDIX   *page* 228

ILLUSTRATIONS

Map of Communications	*page* 10
Bamboo huts in an Eastern Pakistan village	*facing page* 78
Brick cottages of a neat and clean village in England	78
Bullocks slowly dragging a wooden plough	79
A tractor-drawn triple-share steel plough works twenty times as fast	79
In Pakistan reaping by hand is slow	142
A 'combine harvester' reaps, threshes, and loads the grain in one operation	142
It takes this man twenty minutes to saw through a log	143
An electric circular saw can do the same work in a few seconds	143
Exports, 1949–50	194
Imports, 1949–50	195
Agricultural map	233
Map showing Pakistan on the Globe	*Endpapers*

CHAPTER I

A SACRED TRUST

WHAT a grand thing it is to be young in a young country like Pakistan. Yet we are old enough to remember the day on which it was proclaimed a free and equal Member of the British Commonwealth of Nations, and we feel old enough to wish we could learn all about our land and play our full part in building its prosperity. We have the opportunity of preparing our whole lives for that purpose. Before us lie many years which we can spend in training for useful careers as citizens of this new State, and, we hope, still more years in which to serve its best interests.

It was on 15 August 1947 that our Pakistan was created. Before that date it had formed part of British India. For nearly fifty years the people of the Indian sub-continent had asked to be given their freedom so that they could govern themselves as they wished. The 400 million inhabitants of the sub-continent had, however, never been one single nation. They really consisted of two distinct nations who had lived there side by side for many centuries, but who had never become merged into each other in spirit or in outlook.

Although physically resembling each other, the two main sections were irreconcilably apart in the most important of all respects : their religions were fundamentally different. On the one hand there were nearly 300 million Hindus; on the other were roughly 90 million Muslims. The Hindus worship many gods in many different forms;

the Muslims believe that there is one and only one God. The Hindus built up a religious caste system; Islam was based upon the universal brotherhood of man. Between these two cardinal doctrines there could be no half-way meeting-place. Each had given rise to its own cultural system. The two might and did touch at some points, but only as oil and water flow together, without mingling.

For about 150 years both Hindus and Muslims had continued to live in the same sub-continent, side by side, yet separate, under British rule. Before the coming of the British, both had in turn established mighty empires in India. With the spread of education and enlightenment in the second half of the nineteenth century and the beginning of the twentieth century, the two sections had striven jointly to throw off the foreign domination by peaceful means, and to govern their own country by themselves. They were given various reforms, by which they gained some share in the work of government; but the complete freedom which they desired seemed always far away and incomplete. The reason was that the Legislative Councils and the Governments of British India were never responsible to the people of India alone. The government was carried on by the authority of the British Parliament, which was not elected by Indians, but by the people of Britain. The country was thus under foreign rule.

Two World Wars, however, and the spread of education in India, together with the proved ability of Indians in the task of administration, caused a gradual change in the attitude of the British Parliament. It was realized that the time had arrived to give India complete self-government. Yet there were difficulties. In the interval between the two World Wars (that is, between the years

1918 and 1939) important changes had come about in the political aims of the Hindus and Muslims. The former had all along preferred a purely unitary system of democracy, with common constituencies for both Hindus and Muslims. Since the Hindus in general outnumbered the Muslims by a ratio of ten votes to three, it was evident that no Muslim would have a chance of being elected to a legislative chamber except in some areas where the Muslims were in a clear majority. Elsewhere the seats were sure to be filled by Hindus.

This might not have mattered so greatly if the Congress had been prepared to show a spirit of equality and tolerance. They proved the contrary, for they turned their backs on agreements which they had made earlier. For instance, by the 1916 Lucknow Pact between the Indian National Congress and the Muslim League, the Congress had recognized the Muslim demand for separate electorates; in 1928, however, the Congress rejected Mr. Jinnah's famous 'Fourteen Points', which included separate communal representation and other safeguards for the protection of Muslim religion, culture, and progress.

Meanwhile, it had become evident that the Congress were aiming at making themselves alone the permanently supreme power in India. They were determined, for example, to by-pass the Urdu language, because it contained some words of Islamic origin. Some Hindu leaders launched the *Shudi* (reconversion of Muslims) and the *Sangathan* (Hindu unity) movements. Bitterness was increased by a series of tragic riots.

At the Round Table Conferences in London between 1930 and 1934, Congress refused to give way on the question of adequate safeguards for the Muslims. The British Prime Minister eventually in 1935 gave his 'Communal Award', in which practically all the demands of the Muslims were recognized and granted—including separate electorates, statutory safeguards for minority rights, communal 'weightage' in the majority provinces, and the creation of Sind as a province. The 1935 Reforms included these items, but the Congress Party continued its pro-Hindu methods, and put into action many schemes which the Muslims considered oppressive.

If such was to be the 'Ram Raj' proclaimed and practised by the Congress, there is no wonder that Muslim reaction took the form of 'Pakistan'. Mr. Mohammed Ali Jinnah had ardently accepted this ideal, and he now united the Muslim masses into its support through the All-India Muslim League. In 1940 the League openly demanded the separation of the Muslim-majority provinces of the Punjab, Sind, the N.W.F.P., Baluchistan, and Bengal from the rest of India, and their regrouping as an independent State under the name of Pakistan ('Land of the Pure'), which had been used for the first time in January 1933 by a Muslim students' society in London. In 1940, 'Pakistan had become the goal of the Mussalmans of India'.

As was to be expected, the Congress bitterly opposed any such plan to partition India. The outbreak of the Second World War halted the march towards independence, and it was not until peace returned that the strength of Muslim sentiment could be proved. In 1946 the League made the demand for Pakistan the chief issue for the first post-war elections. The result was a clear manifestation of the will of the Muslim people. The League won all the 30 Muslim seats in the Central Legislative Assembly and 427 out of 507 seats in the Provincial Assemblies.

Efforts by the British Government to end the deadlock between League and Congress failed until Lord Mountbatten was sent to India as Viceroy in March 1947 with orders to come to a final settlement. The Congress now realized that the creation of Pakistan was inevitable and gave up its opposition to the idea. On 2 June 1947, Lord Mountbatten announced his plan, which set up Pakistan as we know it to-day. On 18 July 1947, the British Parliament passed the Indian Independence Act, laying down that: 'From 15 August 1947, two independent Dominions shall be set up in India to be known as India and Pakistan'. Even though he had not gained all his original hopes, Mr. Jinnah had won a stupendous triumph, for which he had fought for over a quarter of a century. It is to his masterly leadership and persistence and to the loyal support of the Muslim masses under the Muslim League that we owe the freedom which we enjoy to-day in our own land.

Such then in brief form has been the story of the creation of our country. Although many of our fellow-Muslims are scattered over different parts of Bharat, the great majority of Muslims have been given the certainty of being able to live according to their own way of life and have been freed from the fear of becoming a permanent subordinate minority. In Pakistan they have a modern Islamic democratic State in which they can preserve their religion and their culture and stand on terms of absolute equality with the rest of the world. They are able, too, to prove that they truly believe and fully observe 'the principles of democracy, freedom, equality, tolerance, and social justice, as enunciated by Islam'—guaranteeing the fundamental rights of all citizens.

The main ideas on which the Constitution of Pakistan as a 'Sovereign Democratic State' are based are clearly proclaimed in the 'Objectives Resolution' moved by the Prime Minister, Mr. Liaquat Ali Khan, in the Constituent Assembly on 7 March 1949, and unanimously adopted by that body, as follows:

In the name of Allah, the Beneficent, the Merciful;

Whereas sovereignty over the entire universe belongs to God Almighty alone and the authority which He has delegated to the State of Pakistan through its people for being exercised within the limit prescribed by Him is a sacred trust;

This Constituent Assembly representing the people of Pakistan resolves to frame a constitution for the Sovereign Independent State of Pakistan;

Wherein the State shall exercise its powers and authority through the chosen representatives of the people;

Wherein the principles of democracy, freedom, equality, tolerance, and social justice, as enunciated by Islam, shall be fully observed;

Wherein the Muslims shall be enabled to order their lives in the individual and collective spheres in accord with the teachings and requirements of Islam as set out in the Holy Quran and the Sunna;

Wherein adequate provision shall be made for the minorities freely to profess and practise their religions and develop their cultures;

Whereby the territories now included in or in accession with Pakistan and such other territories as may hereafter be included in or accede to Pakistan shall form a Federation wherein the units will be autonomous with such boundaries and limitations on their powers and authority as may be prescribed;

Wherein shall be guaranteed fundamental rights including equality of status, of opportunity and before law, social, economic, and political justice, and freedom of thought, expression, faith, worship, and association, subject to law and public morality;

Wherein adequate provision shall be made to safeguard the legitimate interests of minorities and backward and depressed classes;

Wherein the independence of the judiciary shall be fully secured;

Wherein the integrity of the territories of the Federation, its independence, and all its rights, including the sovereign rights on land, sea, and air shall be safeguarded;

So that the people of Pakistan may prosper and attain their rightful and honoured place among the nations of the world and make their full contribution towards international peace and the progress and happiness of humanity.

In obedience to this Objectives Resolution, the work of planning all the many details of the Constitution (which means really the 'set-up' of our country and how its affairs will be managed) has been proceeding. Meanwhile, a Provisional Government has carried on the control of public affairs until the Constitution is ready and becomes law. The Provisional Government has thus been only a temporary system. It has consisted of the Governor-General, who is appointed by the King of England on the recommendation of the Pakistan Prime Minister, his Council of Ministers, and the Constituent Assembly as the Federal Parliament. The parts of the Federation are the four Governor's Provinces (Eastern Bengal, the Western Punjab, the North-West Frontier Province, and Sind), each with its own Governor, its own Council of Ministers, and its own Legislative Assembly.

From the date of the creation of our country we have

watched with wonder and interest the prodigious efforts that are being made to bring greater contentment and happiness to our people everywhere. There were enormous early difficulties to be overcome. In the first few months millions of Muslim refugees poured into Pakistan from Bharat and from Kashmir. Their sufferings had to be relieved and work or land provided for them. At the same time we had to place our Defence Forces on a sound footing, and prepare vast plans to increase the prosperity of our people.

Fortunately, we possessed in our beloved Quaid-i-Azam the wisest and most devoted of leaders, whose life was spared long enough for the early problems to be solved. He received most loyal and courageous support from the leading statesmen and administrators. Their work has prospered, and we are inspired by their noble example. We feel that we too can do our bit to make our country great and happy. But first we have to learn very much about Pakistan and all the things that remain to be done. This book tells us about our country, the life of its people, and the ways in which they are striving to uplift themselves. When we have read these chapters we shall have succeeded in our first task, which is to understand our needs and our glorious opportunities.

CHAPTER II

FIVE THOUSAND YEARS OF HISTORY

PAKISTAN became a free and self-governing Member of the British Commonwealth on 15 August 1947. It has thus only just begun its life as a modern country. It has had only a few years' existence as a separate State. It would be completely wrong to say, however, that its history covers only those few brief years. Pakistan's known history goes back to over five thousand years ago.

Although the 'youngest' of the world's independent countries to-day, it is one of the 'oldest'. That may appear a strange contradiction. Nevertheless, we know far more about Western Pakistan as it was in 2500 B.C. than about Western Europe or North America of that same age. The evidence of history is that there were civilized people living in well-planned cities along the banks of the Indus River at a time when the countries now known as Britain, France, Germany, and the United States were occupied only by primitive tribes who sheltered in caves and forests.

Four or five thousand years ago, men had not learned to write; yet they left much evidence about the kind of lives they led. Cave dwellings have been found in many parts of the world. In and around them, though for long ages hidden by the soil, have been discovered the rough stone tools and weapons which they used. Historians have examined these carefully and compared them with other specimens, and are able to tell us that the people who

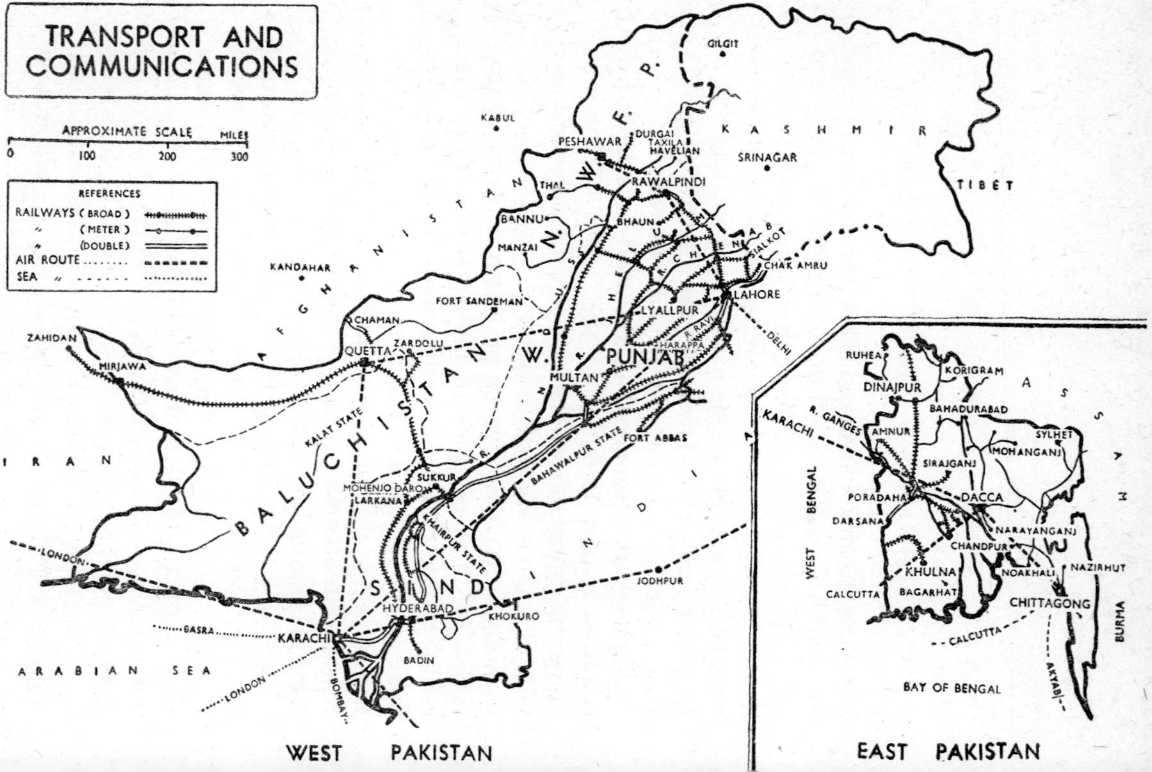
TRANSPORT AND COMMUNICATIONS
APPROXIMATE SCALE
MILES
0
100
200
300
REFERENCES
RAILWAYS (BROAD)
" (METER)
" (DOUBLE)
AIR ROUTE
SEA "
KABUL
KANDAHAR
AFGHANISTAN
PESHAWAR
DURGAI
TAXILA
HAVELIAN
RAWALPINDI
THAL
BANNU
MANZAI
N. W. F. P.
GILGIT
KASHMIR
SRINAGAR
TIBET
BHAUN
SIALKOT
CHAK AMRU
LAHORE
DELHI
LYALLPUR
R. RAVI
HARAPPA
PUNJAB
W.
MULTAN
FORT SANDEMAN
CHAMAN
ZAHIDAN
MIRJAWA
QUETTA
ZARDOLU
BALUCHISTAN
KALAT STATE
IRAN
FORT ABBAS
BAHAWALPUR STATE
INDIA
SUKKUR
MOHENJO DARO
LARKANA
KHAIRPUR STATE
SIND
JODHPUR
HYDERABAD
KHOKURO
BADIN
KARACHI
BASRA
LONDON
BOMBAY
ARABIAN SEA
WEST PAKISTAN
RUHEA
KORIGRAM
DINAJPUR
BAHADURABAD
R. GANGES
AMNUR
KARACHI
SYLHET
MOHANGANJ
SIRAJGANJ
ASSAM
WEST BENGAL
PORADAHA
DACCA
DARSANA
NARAYANGANJ
CHANDPUR
KHULNA
NOAKHALI
NAZIRHUT
CALCUTTA
BAGARHAT
CHITTAGONG
BURMA
CALCUTTA
BAY OF BENGAL
AKYAB
EAST PAKISTAN

lived in Quetta, probably before 3000 B.C., were no longer savages.

Near Quetta are five mounds of earth which were once the sites of ancient villages. Digging there, historians have come across fragments of pottery, painted in geometric patterns and very similar to early pottery found in Persia and Asia Minor. There have been further discoveries of a different kind of pottery and some other strange articles, such as copper axes, knives, saws, and chisels, in parts of Sind and Baluchistan. Clay figures, vases, cups, jars, and dishes have been dug up in southern Baluchistan, and the remains of mud-brick houses have been found. Ancient relics have also been discovered in the Zhob River Valley north and north-east of Quetta. The opinion of historians is that roughly 5,000 years ago the western fringe of Western Pakistan was inhabited by small village communities who were no longer ignorant savages, but were somewhat civilized.

It seems probable that about a thousand years later, that is, between 2500 and 1500 B.C., the whole of the long valley of the Indus River, from the foot of the Himalayas to the Arabian Sea, was occupied by people who had a common way of living and who used the same tools, utensils, and ornaments. All along that 1,000 miles valley we find traces of the existence of what must have been one nation who possessed a common civilization. They lived chiefly in small villages and towns, but they also had two very large cities, the remains of which have been dug out and can be clearly seen to-day.

One of these ancient cities is on the right bank of the Indus, about 200 miles north-east of Karachi, at a place named Mohenjo-daro ('Hill of the Dead'). That is the modern name, and we are not certain of the name by which the city was known to the ancient people. About 400 miles farther north-east, and on the left bank of the Ravi River, there are the ruins of another large city, Harappa, only 110 miles south-west of Lahore. For over 3,000 years they had lain buried and forgotten, and were discovered only thirty years ago.

Mohenjo-daro and Harappa were built chiefly of baked bricks, and both cities consisted of two parts—a fortress and an outer residential or business area. Both cities had *bunds* to protect them from floods which evidently took place in those days in the Indus, as now. There were wide streets which were lined with drains. Mohenjo-daro was clearly built according to a definite plan. The houses consisted of a courtyard round which were a number of rooms, but there are few signs of any ornamentation, and the general appearance must have been monotonous. Mohenjo-daro was nearly two and a half miles long and over a mile wide; Harappa was a trifle smaller. They were well-arranged cities, with baths and granaries, showing that the people were fairly advanced and that they possessed an orderly government.

As Mohenjo-daro and Harappa existed long before the Islamic era, their remains of course contain no suggestion of any Muslim associations. Nor among the ruins is there anything that resembles a temple, but there are figures and seals and pottery which indicate that there existed some form of religion. The people themselves were not all of the same race. They wore some clothing and appear to have known how to make cotton cloth. They were of an olive complexion, with dark hair and handsome features. Possibly they looked very like the Spaniards and other Mediterranean races of to-day. In build they were of medium height and slender. Some, however, appear to have been traders from Mongolia and others perhaps were Gonds from southern India.

Who the citizens of those Indus Valley cities and towns really were we cannot guess to-day. Their homes and cities, their ornaments and utensils—these were often very like those objects which have been dug up at the ruins of other ancient cities, such as Ur (in Mesopotamia). Both Mohenjo-daro and Harappa lasted for a few hundred years—and both were suddenly destroyed. From some far-distant part of Asia came a horde of Aryans in about 1500 B.C., and it is thought by historians that they seized Mohenjo-daro and Harappa and massacred the inhabitants. From all the towns and villages in the long Indus Valley the people fled, leaving their homes and their fields to desolation. Thus died the 'Indus Valley Civilization', while the Aryans passed on into the eastern Punjab and the Ganges Valley. Perhaps the Vedic hymns refer to that tragic war of 3,500 years ago, and the destroyer may have been Indra, the Aryan 'war-god'.

There are no written records of the Indus Valley civilization and its end. The *Rigveda* and other Hindu epics were originally verses which were committed to memory, and handed on thus from scholar to scholar and finally 'written' long later.

A thousand miles away and separated from Western Pakistan by the whole width of India, lies our other important territory of Eastern Pakistan. Although much smaller in area, it contains a distinctly larger population than Western Pakistan. In Eastern Pakistan there are 45 million people; in Western Pakistan 35 millions—making a total of 80 millions for the whole of our country.

Although so far away, Eastern Pakistan has for many hundreds of years been closely related to Western

Pakistan. The great majority of its people are Muslims, and therefore have the same way of living and thinking. As we shall see in the next chapter, Eastern and Western Pakistan are in fact one country and one people, separated only by distance and not by mind or spirit. If we do not trace historical events so far back there, it is nevertheless true that Eastern Pakistan (which includes Eastern Bengal and parts of Assam) had a great and important past, and owes its modern greatness partly to the same historical causes.

Returning for a while to the Indus Valley, we find that after the destruction of Mohenjo-daro and Harappa the country became split up into several small kingdoms, whose names were changed from time to time. One of these kingdoms was Gandhara, which roughly covered the same area as is now occupied by Peshawar district and the Kabul River valley. There was also the kingdom of Urasa or Hazara, whose name still exists in the form of the Orash Plain. The ancient kingdom of Tasila was much the same in extent as the present districts of Rawalpindi and Attock.

After the disastrous fall of Mohenjo-daro and Harappa, nearly 1,200 years had to pass before written history arrived. From this source we know that a great Persian king, named Darius, invaded what is now Western Pakistan in 512 B.C., and made the Indus River the eastern boundary of his empire. In 326 B.C. Alexander the Great of Macedonia fought his way with his Greek troops to the banks of the Indus, and there, at Taxila, received the surrender of the Indian king Porus. Alexander advanced as far as the Beas River; but his soldiers grew tired of marching and wanted to return to Greece, which they had not seen for years. They refused

FIVE THOUSAND YEARS OF HISTORY 15

to go any farther, and Alexander was forced to retreat. When he died in 323 B.C. Greek rule came to an end in northern India.

By Alexander's day the age of real history had begun. Knowledge of reading and writing had spread through the then civilized world, and men were thus able to leave real records of events. They wrote brief stories in the form of inscriptions on rocks or on coins and monuments, as well as in the form of books made of strips of palm-leaf or parchment. Trade and travel had linked up Greece and Rome with neighbouring countries, and scholars marched with the armies of the generals. In this way fairly complete knowledge has come to us about the ancient world.

The next to gain mastery in the Indus Valley were Chandra Gupta Maurya and his grandson Asoka, whose capital (Pataliputra) was situated near the present Patna. They were Buddhist emperors. For the next few hundred years the north-west corner of ancient India remained under Buddhist rule. Now and then fresh invaders entered the country through the passes on the west, and there was often much confusion. Among the various conquerors who came and went were the White Huns, the Turki Shahiya kings of Kabul, Arabs, local rajahs, and (in A.D. 986–7) the Turkish Sultan, Sabaktagin, with whose arrival the Islamic Faith obtained its first real footing in the Indian continent.

During the 850 years that followed, the Indus Valley was ruled almost continuously by Muslims. Wave upon wave of invaders, often of completely different origin, occupied the country in turn—Afghans, Turks, Mongols (who, however, were savages and non-Muslim), and finally the Moghals under Babar. The latter set up a great empire, which extended over Afghanistan and nearly the whole of India, and which lasted for about 400 years under famous rulers like Akbar, Jahangir, Shahjahan, and Aurangzeb. Kashmir was brought under Moghal sway by Akbar, who conquered that region in 1587.

By the middle of the seventeenth century, however, new invasions weakened the power of the Moghals. Nadir Shah, a Turkman shepherd who had made himself King of Persia, sacked Delhi. His successors and Ahmad Shah (Durani) also overran the country. Meanwhile, the Sikhs, with the support of the Muslims, had gained in strength, and they grew so powerful under Rangit Singh that they became the rulers of the Punjab from 1764 to 1849. The Sikhs in turn were defeated by the British, who in 1849 annexed the country and made it into a Province of India. The coming of the British was welcomed by the Muslims, who for the next ninety-eight years remained mostly on good terms with the East India Company and the British Government—until the great act of freedom of 1947 separated Pakistan from non-Muslim India and established it as a self-governing Member of the British Commonwealth.

CHAPTER III

THE TWO PAKISTANS ARE ONE

So far our attention has been fixed mainly upon the area which is now known as Western Pakistan. This is only natural, because here was the centre of the vast Muslim Empire of the Moghals, with Lahore, Agra, or Delhi as the capital. This, however, does not mean that Eastern Pakistan counted for nothing. On the contrary, even the earlier Afghan rulers regarded Bengal as an important part of their possessions, and placed the province under their Viceroys. Many Muslim families settled there, and large numbers of the local population accepted the faith of Islam, enjoying for several hundred years the peace and prosperity which Moghal rule brought to those parts. The last of the Hindu kings fled before the advance of the victorious Muslim armies under the famous general Bukhtiyar Khilji, and the Emperor Alauddin in 1299 made Sonargaon the seat of Muslim government in Eastern Bengal. The town later became a great religious centre.

Later, with the arrival of the Moghals, Sonargaon lost importance and Dacca rose to fame. Dacca, then a mere village, occupies a strategic position near the meeting-place of two navigable rivers. It quickly became the capital of the province under Islam Khan, who had been made Viceroy in 1608. A few years later the port of Chittagong, even then well known for its good harbour and its extensive trade, came under Moghal rule. For a short time Rajmahal became the capital, but Dacca regained its supremacy.

It was during this interval, however, that the English first gained a footing in Eastern Bengal, being granted a *nishan* in 1651 to establish a trading station (known as a 'factory') at Rajmahal. Shortly afterwards the Muslim army conquered Cooch Behar and parts of Assam. Under the famous Viceroy, Shaista Khan, Eastern Bengal was the scene of even greater Moghal successes. His fleet destroyed the Mugh pirates, who had long preyed upon peaceful shipping in the Ganges delta. Shaista Khan next conquered Chittagong, which he annexed permanently to the Kingdom of Bengal. Peace having been established everywhere in the province, a rich trade sprang up, with Dacca as its centre—muslin and silk being exported to Europe; coral, amber, and tortoiseshell to Bhutan, Assam, and Siam; rice to the Coromandel coast (at the amazingly cheap price of 640 lb. to the rupee). It was during this era that Dacca muslin became famous all over the world.

After Shaista Khan's retirement, trouble broke out with the East India Company. The latter were looking for a suitable place in which to establish a trading centre in Bengal. The Emperor Aurangzeb, however, was angry with the English for having fortified Madras and Bombay against his orders, and for having allied themselves with his enemies the Marathas. At his command the English agents at Dacca were flung into prison and the English trading fleet sailed away. In 1690 Job Charnock, the East India Company's representative, landed at the tiny village of Sutanati, on the Hooghly River, and there set up a trading centre which later grew into the mighty city of Calcutta. Not long afterwards, the Moghal Viceroy left Dacca, which ceased to be the capital of Bengal. The decline of Moghal power had now begun and in 1766, as the result of Clive's victory at the battle of Plassey (1757), the English occupied Dacca by right of a treaty by which the Dewani of Bengal, Bihar, and Orissa had been handed to the Company.

For the next 140 years Dacca remained one of the 'forgotten cities' of the Indian continent. From being the capital of a large province, it became merely the headquarters of a division. Its industries had declined, and it was known in Bengal as only a rather busy market town with a large trade in rice and jute. It was not until 1905 that the city regained some of its lost importance. In that year Bengal was partitioned by Lord Curzon (Viceroy) in such a way that the three divisions of Chittagong, Dacca, and Rajshahi were handed over along with Assam (previously a Chief Commissionership) to form a new province, known as 'Eastern Bengal and Assam', under a Lieutenant-Governor.

This was a measure of great significance to the Muslims of those parts, for in the new province they numbered eighteen millions, as compared with only twelve million Hindus. The Muslims thus suddenly found themselves in the majority, with Dacca restored to its position as the capital of a large province. There was great rejoicing, except among the Hindu lawyers and journalists who immediately started an angry agitation. They made bitter attacks on Sir Bamfylde Fuller, who was appointed first Lieutenant-Governor of the new province, and who did his best to make the partition a success.

With the establishment of their own High Court, Government offices, colleges, and other fine buildings, a new pride was felt among the people of Dacca. The city was no longer content to be dragged at the tail of Calcutta. A new and independent spirit sprang up. Even though the partition was cancelled by the Royal Proclamation of the King Emperor in person at the Delhi Coronation Durbar in 1911, and Dacca thereby again ceased to be a capital and became once more only the headquarters of a division, the seeds of a grand ambition had been sown. Not only Dacca, but Chittagong also, felt the benefits of those six brief years of the partition. Trade increased; rail and river communications were improved; the demand for education spread everywhere; better crops of rice and jute were raised; old industries were revived and new ones were introduced.

Thirty-six years were to pass before a still greater partition took place. That was in 1947, when the whole Indian continent was divided between the Pakistan Dominion and the Indian Republic. That historic event, which meant the end of British rule, again restored Dacca to its position as the capital of a province—this time as the chief city of Eastern Pakistan, under a Governor. Today, with its own University, High Court, and Secretariat, Eastern Pakistan sees the fulfilment of many noble dreams.

The whole area has quickly benefited. Chittagong's importance as a trading port has enormously increased. United by their religious faith and their own *raj,* the people of Eastern Pakistan are full of high hopes for the future. They occupy a strategic position of great importance, for they are close neighbours to the rapidly progressing millions of China and Burma.

There is a strange geographical similarity between Eastern and Western Pakistan, for both regions guard the land frontiers at the two extremities of the Indian con-

THE TWO PAKISTANS ARE ONE

tinent. The safety of the latter, indeed, depends largely upon the prosperity, strength, and valour of the two Pakistan zones: the West holding the passes against Russia and Afghanistan; the East watching the activities of Burmans and Chinese. Both our regions produce goods which are in great demand throughout the world—cotton, wheat, and minerals in Western Pakistan; jute, tea, timber, and rice in Eastern Pakistan. Both too are peopled mainly by believers in the same faith, with the same way of life. They stand firmly together. Even if separated by distance, they are complementary to each other. They are indeed a single country, alive, free, and indivisible—the 'Land of the Pure'.

CHAPTER IV

OUR PEOPLE AND THEIR CUSTOMS

Owing to the many invasions of the country which is now known as Pakistan, we cannot rightly think of our people as belonging to one distinct and separate race, in the same sense as, for example, the Scottish, the Irish, or the English. These last three have remained in their own proper countries for many hundreds of years and, although people from other lands have settled and intermarried there from time to time, the English, Irish, and Scottish have undergone little change in appearance or character since a long time ago. Similarly, other nations, like the Japanese or the Portuguese, have remained distinct for many generations.

In a previous chapter we learnt that many kinds of invaders poured into India through the north-west passes. The new-comers often belonged to quite different racial stocks, with very little in common between them. There were Indo-Aryans, Greeks, Persians, Afghans, Arabs, Moghals, Semitics. Several of these big invasions took place within the last 1,000 years. The result has been a great intermixture of races, for the conquerors in each case settled down and lived for a long time in north-west India.

It is not unusual to find a nation with so much mixture of blood. The United States to-day is a striking example of how a powerful nation can be created out of widely different stocks. The Americans came from Britain, France, Italy, Germany, Norway, Finland, and many

OUR PEOPLE AND THEIR CUSTOMS 23

other countries of Europe during the past 250 years. Among them also we find several million Negroes who were originally slaves brought from Africa. The immigrants brought with them to the United States many widely different languages, but found it most convenient to use English, which is their common tongue to-day. They also belonged to different religions and sects—Christian and Jewish. They had their own separate customs and ideas. In spite of all these differences they were very quickly able to mingle everything in one common lot and call themselves Americans, with full loyalty to the United States, obeying one law, one Government, and one social system.

We Pakistanis are somewhat like the Americans in that respect. We have descended from a number of different races and origins, but have so much in common with each other through living permanently in one region that we see no real difference in each other. We share one patriotic devotion. We all use more or less one common language and our customs are very much alike.

The great majority of our people, both in Western Pakistan and in Eastern Pakistan, are Muslims. This is a great bond between us, for it means that we have one religion and one way of life. Wherever we go in our country, from Sylhet in the distant east to Quetta in the extreme west, we nearly all of us worship God in the same way, believe in the teachings of the Holy Quran, and obey a single code of conduct. This creates a tremendous feeling of 'oneness' among our people. The Muslim from Kohat may enter the house of a fellow-Muslim in Chittagong and feel completely as if it were his own home. His mosques look alike and the prayers are exactly the same. There are the familiar feast days, the same thoughts spoken in the sermons. We know from this that we are a single brotherhood. When we add to this the knowledge that we live in a free and independent country together, we realize that we are in fact a nation. Each person, each family, each community is equally important to all the rest; the welfare of one is the concern of all.

Although Muslims are by far the most numerous among us, we also know that there are some non-Muslims who, in spite of a difference in religion or racial descent, share our country and care for it as much as Muslims do. They and their forefathers have lived in it for perhaps hundreds of years. In Pakistan they hold their land and carry on their daily work. They could have gone away (as so many millions of others did) when India was partitioned, but they preferred to remain of their own free will. We welcome their presence, for they are good and useful citizens, obeying our laws and helping our country in many ways. We treat them as equals and as fellow-countrymen.

A person can be a good Pakistani, whether he is Muslim or non-Muslim. There are no barriers or obstacles to the comfort and happiness of the Pakistani non-Muslim. It is enough for us to know that he is a loyal Pakistani. He can take up any work he pleases or be admitted equally into our Armed Forces or the Government services. He is free to trade, cultivate his land, travel, worship according to the teachings of his own religion, marry, send his children to school, and receive the full protection of the law. Nobody interferes with his rights as a citizen. All the citizens of Pakistan are free and equal in our eyes.

Among the non-Muslim citizens of our country we

should specially name the Hindus, the Parsees, and the Christians. When the Census is taken in 1951, it will be possible to say how many there are of each. The Census is a careful counting of our country's population, in towns and villages alike, class by class and tribe by tribe, with their occupations and many other details. A Census is usually held once in every ten years. As Pakistan was created only in 1947, and many more important things had to be done first, it has only now been possible to arrange a full Census.

Meanwhile, we can make a fair guess. The 1941 Census helps slightly, but we have to remember that millions of Hindus and Sikhs left for Bharat in 1947 and millions of Muslims came to us from Bharat. It is probably close to the real figures if we say that there are a little over 80 million men, women, and children living in Pakistan to-day. Of these, the Muslims number about 68 million. There are about 11 million Hindus, 400,000 Christians, and 5,000 Parsees. Nearly all the Sikhs crossed into Bharat.

Our 68 million Muslims are made up of a large number of different tribes. Chief among them are Jats, who are fine soldiers and excellent cultivators, and who live mostly in the western Punjab. In the south-west of Western Pakistan and parts of Sind we find the Baluchis, a manly and honest people who are often splendid horsemen. The North-West Frontier Province and the districts of Attock and Miamwali contain mostly Pathans, who are brave and dashing soldiers and excellent workmen. Living side by side with them are large numbers of Awans and Shekhs. The Aroras form the trading classes. There are several other tribes. The arrival of millions of Muslim refugees from the Eastern Punjab, Delhi, and the

United Provinces has meant changes and the opening of new settlements in many parts of Western Pakistan. Large numbers have been given land in Sind.

In Western Pakistan the Hindus who have remained are to be found chiefly in the big cities of Karachi and Lahore. There are about 250,000 Hindu cultivators left in Sind. The Parsees are nearly all in Karachi. The Christians are scattered in small communities throughout the land, where they have their own churches and missions. Among the Christians are the Anglo-Indians, who live chiefly in Lahore and Karachi, and who are useful members of the Government, railway, and telegraphic services. Many Anglo-Indians have enlisted in the Armed Forces. At Karachi are also a few hundred Christian Goans, who are of mixed Portuguese descent.

In Eastern Bengal we have about 32 million Muslims and 10 million Hindus, with a few thousand Christians. Although so far distant from the western mountain passes through which Ancient India was invaded, Eastern Pakistan felt the effects of those invasions. The province was directly ruled by Muslims for over 550 years—from A.D. 1200, under the Turki emperors, until 1757, when Clive conquered Eastern Bengal from Nawab Suraj-ud-Dowlah as the result of the Battle of Plassey. In those 550 years many Afghans and Moghals settled there and large Muslim armies were stationed in the districts. Millions of the local population became converts to Islam, and they have always remained very devoted Muslims. There are more mosques in Dacca than in any other city of the Indian continent. Most of Eastern Bengal's Muslims, however, are cultivators, labourers, boatmen, and cottage industrialists.

The Hindus consist almost entirely of Bengalis, most

of whom belong to the four higher castes. They have the right of observing their religious practices. In the Provincial Legislative Assembly they have 46 seats (28 for Caste Hindus and 18 for the Scheduled Castes) out of a total house of 171 seats. While the majority of Bengali Hindus are cultivators or labourers, many are traders, teachers, and Government servants. They are given exactly the same rights as all other members of the Dominion of Pakistan—equal protection, equal justice, equal opportunity, and equal freedom, and all the other benefits of a modern democratic State, in obedience to the principles of Islam.

Pakistan, taken as a whole, is a land of villages and market towns. There are only five big cities—Karachi, Lahore, Dacca, Peshawar, and Chittagong. More than nine out of ten of its people are directly concerned with the cultivation of fields or the rearing of animals. As large parts of the country, especially in Western Pakistan, have not yet been brought under cultivation, it is only natural that the population should be unevenly distributed. Thus, while the density of population (that is, the number of people per square mile) is heavy in the western Punjab because of the network of canals which water the fields, it is very light in other regions, such as in parts of the Thal and Sind Deserts, where rainfall and canal water are still very scarce. Great new irrigation schemes are being planned all along the Indus Valley; when these are completed, several million acres will be turned into fertile fields for wheat, cotton, and other crops, and new settlers will help to increase the density of population in those regions. There are also irrigation plans for Baluchistan. On an average there are about 109 persons per square mile in Western Pakistan.

Eastern Pakistan is already blessed with abundant rainfall, and much of the province is well cultivated. As a result the population is much denser (870 persons per square mile) than in Western Pakistan. Eastern Bengal is, in fact, one of the most thickly inhabited regions in the whole world. Four-fifths of its whole area is under various crops. When the remaining land is also brought under cultivation and the quality of the grain crops is improved, the province will be able to support many millions more people.

Both in population and in size Pakistan is one of the largest countries in the world. It is easily the largest of the Islamic countries: Turkey comes second with seventeen millions; Egypt third with sixteen millions. There are only four other countries with a larger population, as the following comparison shows:—

		Millions
1.	China	454·00
2.	Bharat (including States)	330·00
3.	U.S.S.R.	170·00
4.	U.S.A.	131·66
5.	Pakistan	80·00
6.	Japan	78·00
7.	Germany	59·00
8.	U.K.	48·00
9.	Italy	45·00
10.	Brazil	42·00

There are also more people living in Pakistan than the total white population of the rest of the British Commonwealth combined. Canada, Australia, and South Africa are bigger Dominions in area, but their populations are considerably smaller. At the same time we must remember that we are a newly created State, whereas these are far older. They have built up great traditions and have long been flourishing countries. Yet our people and our resources are as good. It rests in our own hands to advance as carefully and as smoothly towards the same goal of national prosperity and contentment. It is entirely in our own power to make a completely happy land of Pakistan.

CHAPTER V

WHAT SELF-GOVERNMENT MEANS

Before we examine just how the task of governing our country is carried out, let us for a short while think about the different ways in which the affairs of a nation can be managed.

In very olden times, when the people of the world were scattered about in the form of large families or tribes, it was very natural that each group should look upon the wisest or strongest man as their chief. We see the same thing even among wild animals, whose herds or packs are usually led by the biggest and most cunning among them. When danger threatens, it is he who turns to face the enemy, and the remainder instinctively follow and obey him.

Among the old tribes, it was the custom also to give the leading warrior a special rank above all the others. In the case of a big tribe or group of tribes, he would be regarded as a king. He used perhaps to listen to the advice of other experienced warriors, but it was really his own will that carried most weight. If he gave an order, it was generally obeyed by all. It was in his power to punish or to reward as he pleased. Nobody dared to challenge his authority. That method of one-man rule over a tribe or country was known as 'autocracy'—government by the will of one man. If he was a king he was called an 'absolute monarch'. If he was not a king he was called a 'dictator'.

In other cases, however, it became the custom for the members of the tribe or nation to choose their own king or chieftain. Some would prefer one particular warrior; some another. They would agree that it would be foolish to fight each other, and so they would decide to meet in a common place; then the leader who was seen to have the largest number of followers would be declared king. Each member of the tribe would 'vote' by raising his spear or striking his shield with his sword when his own hero's name was called. The biggest number of votes was what counted. Once chosen, it was to him that all would give their support and loyalty.

We go through something like the same process to-day when we elect (or choose) our football or cricket captain. For example, all the boys of our school or all our club members hold a meeting. There they find that three or four names are mentioned as being the best or cleverest players. As there can be only one captain, each member puts his mark against the name of the candidate whom he thinks to be the most suitable. In this way all are able to vote. The votes are then counted, and the player with the largest number of votes is declared to have been elected captain. Having made their choice, all the members of the club or team trust him and obey his orders on the field.

A captain usually has a few other experienced players to help him with advice or to take up special tasks. In the case of a very large school or club, he cannot conveniently do everything himself. He needs someone to keep the lists of members, to write letters, and attend to various other matters; someone else to collect the subscriptions and make the payments; a third person perhaps to arrange the matches. Then there are usually four or five others whose advice is valuable. In this way the captain has several helpers who take part in running the club and in drawing up or coaching the teams. All these people, taken together, are known as a committee. Each office-holder is elected by the entire body of club members.

The affairs of a country are much greater than a club's business, and a very large number of questions of all kinds have to be dealt with. It would be very rare for even an extremely wise king to know how everything should be arranged, and to see to the proper government of his country single-handed. An absolute monarch used to appoint his office-holders (or ministers) himself. In times of danger, or when anything special had to be done, he would often think it better to call the whole tribe together to advise him and to make their own wishes known.

As tribes grew bigger and became nations, their king would find it impossible to hold a meeting of the whole nation at the same time in one place. He would therefore ask for only the wisest men to come from each town or district. Then the various towns and villages would hold their own meetings, at which they would decide (by voting) who were their wisest local leaders. The men so chosen would go as their representatives to the chief city (or capital), where they would meet together and tell the king and his ministers what the people in the towns and villages thought about the different problems of the whole country. Such a gathering of the elected wise men is known as a parliament.

The good government of a country is divided into three main tasks. First of all there have to be the general rules which all have to obey. Then there must be laws to show what a man can do or cannot do. For example, he cannot be allowed to kill or injure other people; nor to steal the

WHAT SELF-GOVERNMENT MEANS

belongings of others; nor to let his cattle loose to feed on his neighbour's wheat; nor to sell things that are harmful. There have to be laws also to show what actions he must perform to help his country and be a good citizen. For example, he must always try to prevent others from committing crimes; he must pay his taxes; he must send his children to school in places where he is required to do so; he must allow others to use the public roads and wells; he must help to prevent sickness.

These are all simple things which we understand easily. But in a nation's life there are many other items which are more difficult to describe. For instance, a person cannot to be allowed to go around spreading falsehoods about someone else, or to cheat his customers, or to be so careless in matters of health as to spread illness, or to make and pass bad coins. We know that these things are wrong and harmful. In order that all people should understand their rights and duties, the country must be given clear and just laws. The making of laws is called 'legislation'. The meeting of wise men who make the laws is known as the 'Legislature' or 'Parliament' (sometimes also called 'Legislative Council' or 'Legislative Assembly').

Law-making, however, is not enough by itself to keep a nation contented and prosperous. There must be people whose special business it is to see that the laws are obeyed. If a man steals or kills, there must be people to find him and place him on trial. If a citizen has to pay taxes, he must be told the amount of money due from him and to whom he must make payment. If his children have to go to school, there must be proper arrangements to supply the schools and teachers and draw up the best courses of study. If he needs water for his fields, canals or wells have to be constructed in places where rainfall is scanty. Railways have to be run properly to enable him to travel. In case of illness, doctors and hospitals must be ready to look after the sick and to prevent the spread of epidemics like plague, cholera, and smallpox.

There are indeed a great many things that have to be done in a modern country to make sure of the happiness and well-being of the people and to arrange for the proper observance of the laws. That part of the work of government is known as 'administration', or the 'executive function'.

When making the laws, therefore, the Legislature also has to arrange for the setting up of suitable Administrative Departments, with trained officials, entrusted with clear duties which they have to carry out in a fair and businesslike manner. At the head of each big Department (or group of Departments) is a Minister chosen from the Legislature. Each Minister has the help of well-qualified Secretaries, Directors, Superintendents, Inspectors, clerks, and other officials. There must also be the Defence Forces (the Army, the Air Force, and the Navy) to keep the country safe against any foreign enemies. All this costs money, for the various officials and even the humblest public servants have to receive fair wages, while all kinds of stores, machinery, and buildings have to be provided.

In Pakistan, which is a modern State, we have Ministers in charge of: Defence; the nation's money matters (Finance); Education, Industries, and Commerce; Food, Agriculture, and Health; Communications; Foreign Affairs; Interior, etc.; Law and Labour.

At the head of these Ministers, and completing the 'Cabinet', is the Prime Minister, who may be in charge of some particular Department, but who is also concerned with each, and who is kept informed of all of them and helps to unify their arrangements. The Ministry or Cabinet is also known as the 'Executive'; it sees to the execution or carrying out of the laws.

There is a third important part of the Government system in any modern country. Sometimes the laws are not easy to understand. Their wording may not be clear enough and disputes can arise as to the real meaning. In such cases there has to be a body of judges to decide what is the correct meaning. These judges do not make the laws; they do not see to the carrying out of the laws; they only interpret and explain the laws and make them clear to all.

In addition, when the laws are broken, the offenders must be given a fair and impartial trial. For this purpose there are courts of justice, with magistrates or judges, before whom all the evidence is placed—whether for or against the offenders. The facts are carefully examined there, and every argument is patiently heard. Sometimes a jury of twelve men helps the judge. No person, accused of an offence, is presumed to be guilty; his guilt has to be proved by clear evidence and truthful witnesses. No outside interference of any kind is allowed. If the parties to any action or suit are not satisfied with the decision or verdict of a lower court, they have the right to appeal to a higher court or to the High Court itself.

The scales of justice are held even. Neither wealth nor position, birth nor private feelings can influence the magistrates and judges. They are concerned only with the truth, and they decide the rights and wrongs of every case according to the law of the land. Although appointed by the Government and paid by the Government, they are completely independent of the Government in the proper discharge of their duties, and cannot be removed for any cause as long as their conduct remains good.

This side of the Government of a country is known as the Judiciary. In Pakistan the strictest care is taken to make sure that every citizen receives the benefit of pure justice. Rich or poor, ignorant or educated, prince or peasant, official or ordinary citizen, man or woman or child, foreigner or Pakistani, Muslim or non-Muslim—every single person in Pakistan has the full protection of the courts of justice, in every corner of the land, and to equal degree.

There remains one more feature of importance which shows how fully the ordinary citizen shares in the work of governing our country. From ancient times the people of our towns and villages have been accustomed to managing their own purely local affairs themselves. In the case of the villages, there have always been *panchayats*, elected by the inhabitants. Similarly, for a long time towns and cities have had their own municipal committees, chosen by the local citizens.

These 'local bodies' generally look after the roads, *mêlas* (fairs), schools, market-places, health, housing, and other simple problems within their own boundaries. For such purposes they are able to raise small local taxes and employ their own officials. There is no direct interference from Provincial or Federal (Central) authorities so long as these *panchayats* and municipalities carry out their work according to the general rules laid down. They are given grants of money by the Provincial Governments, and are watched over by the Minister for Local Self-government.

From all these facts it will now have become clear to

WHAT SELF-GOVERNMENT MEANS

us that in Pakistan the citizen plays the biggest part in the management of his country's affairs. It is true that he does not directly make the laws; but he elects the Assembly and Council members who do the actual legislation. They are his representatives, for whom he has voted. It is true also that he does not personally see to the proper carrying out of each and every law; but he pays the taxes out of which come the salaries of the Ministers and officials who do that work in each Department as directed by the elected Assemblies and Councils. He knows also that if the legislative members do not please him, he can vote for others at the next elections. In this way he can make sure of securing the best representatives. There are always many candidates eager to have the honour of being elected to the Assemblies, municipalities, and *panchayats*.

By this means the electors are able to make their wishes clear and to ensure that good laws are made and that the officials discharge their duties well. In Pakistan every grown-up man or woman will have the right to take part in elections. Through this means the will of the people is the real controlling voice in public affairs. Under such a system it is impossible for one individual to become a dictator in Pakistan. The voters have the right to say what is good for the country and who are the most trustworthy representatives to elect. The real power is the vote itself. Through his or her vote, therefore, each citizen helps to govern the whole country for the benefit of all. Such a system is known as Democracy (from the Greek *demos*—people, and *kratein*—to rule)—'government *of* the people, *by* the people, *for* the people'. Pakistan is a Democracy.

CHAPTER VI

AN ASSEMBLY AT WORK

EACH of Pakistan's four provinces has its own Legislative Assembly and its own Executive or Cabinet. These, however, are concerned only with the affairs of the province itself, and do not interfere with each other or with the business of the country as a whole.

A Legislative Assembly is an elected body. It contains a number of seats, each of which is filled by a representative of a particular town or district or of an important body of citizens like a chamber of commerce or a university.

Although the details have not yet been announced, because the making of Pakistan's constitution has not been completed, it seems probable that every man and woman over the age of 21 will have one vote. That is the custom in all modern democratic countries.

As we can well imagine, it is impossible for all the millions of people in any country to meet at the same time in one single place and do their voting. Each province has therefore been divided into a number of electoral districts (known as 'constituencies') in such a way that no place is left out and the districts contain a more or less equal number of voters.

Each electoral area has the right to elect one representative to the Provincial Assembly. Some of the districts are populated chiefly by landholders and farm workers; these are known as rural constituencies. Others consist of the people of large towns, and are known as urban constituencies. The very large cities, like Karachi, Lahore, and Dacca, will probably be divided into several constituencies because of the very large number of voters. It is usual for a constituency to contain about 50,000–80,000 voters.

Let us suppose that a Provincial Assembly contains about 300 seats. When the Assembly is being formed, all these seats have to be filled at the same time. This is done by holding a General Election, at which voting is done in all the constituencies on the same date. The life of an Assembly may last three or five years, after which another General Election would have to be held and all the seats filled again. If an Assembly member dies at any time between two General Elections, his seat is filled by means of a By-election, at which only his constituency is required to vote.

For days before an election there is much excitement in each constituency. The citizens hold meetings, and the leaders of all parties go round making speeches to the voters. The names of the candidates are announced. Generally each party says that its own candidate is the best, and the party leaders carefully explain their policy. The voters listen attentively, ask many questions, and make up their minds as to how they will give their vote. The voters are told their own numbers in the electoral rolls and learn where and when to vote.

Meanwhile, polling stations are being prepared in various parts of each town or village. At the polling stations are the ballot boxes, in which the voting papers will be safely placed. On polling day itself the voters flock to the polling booths, where they find many officials to help them. Each voter is given a paper on which are printed the names of the candidates standing for election from his constituency. If the voter cannot read or write, there will be some drawing or colour by which he can tell which is his own favourite candidate. All that the voter has to do is to write a big black cross in the empty space alongside that candidate's name. Then the voter folds his voting paper and drops it into the box.

All the voting is done secretly. Nobody is allowed to watch the voter to see where he has put his mark. That is what is meant by the words 'Secret Ballot'. In this way every voter is able to choose whatever name he wishes without anybody else knowing. This prevents him from being afraid of the results of voting. It is a punishable offence for any person to try to bribe or threaten a voter. It is also an offence for a person to use another's voting paper. No proxies are allowed.

At the end of the day the ballot boxes are locked and sealed. They are then collected from all the various polling booths and brought to the central office of each constituency. There they are opened in the presence of the chief electoral officer and the candidates, and the votes are counted one by one. The candidate who gains the greatest number of votes is declared elected as the representative of that constituency.

On the day of the first meeting of the Provincial Assembly all the representatives come to the Assembly Chamber from their towns and districts. Each representative has the right to take his seat in some part of the big hall. It is usual for all the members of each party to sit together in their proper groups so as to be able to consult each other.

The Assembly having been declared open, their first duty is to choose the 'Speaker' of the Assembly. It will be his duty to take the president's chair and to see that the debates and the voting in the Chamber are carried out properly according to the usual customs of a democratic gathering. He occupies an important place, for he has to see that all the members have a fair and equal chance to speak, and that the business of the House is carried on peacefully and correctly. He takes no sides, but is impartial and neutral. If the voting in the House is equal, he has the right to give the casting vote. He has the power of suspending any member who breaks the rules. All the members treat him with great respect and obey him.

In the case of a new Assembly, it soon becomes clear which party has the largest number of seats. As all the decisions of the Assembly are by voting, naturally the biggest party will win most of the debates. The Governor of the Province therefore calls upon the leader of the biggest party to 'form the Government'. The leader is given the post of Prime Minister, and he chooses from among his best followers the ten or twelve Ministers who will form his Cabinet. One is placed in charge of Education, another of Finance, a third Health, a fourth Agriculture, and so on—until all the principal Departments have their own Ministers. Each is responsible for the good management of his special Department. The lines on which he is expected to work are decided, however, by the Cabinet as a whole. Every important step is taken after the Ministers have consulted each other in their Cabinet meetings. In this way the policy of the party to which they belong is carried out and the whole Cabinet is held responsible. If any serious mistake is made, it is not only the Minister concerned who is blamed, but the whole Cabinet. This system is known as 'Joint Cabinet Responsibility'.

The Assembly carries on most of its business through the making or changing of the laws, the passing of resolutions, and the asking of questions. When a new law is required, its proposals are placed before the Assembly in the form of a Bill. The Bill is discussed clause by clause, amended where necessary, and voted on three times by the whole House before it is passed. It has then to be signed by the Governor before it becomes an Act, and the consent of the Governor-General has also to be obtained.

A Bill can be introduced by any member of the Assembly and not only by the Cabinet. If the majority of votes is in its favour, it is passed; if most of the votes are against it, the Bill is rejected, and cannot be reintroduced in the lifetime of the same Assembly. Only the Cabinet, however, has the right to introduce a Money Bill, dealing with how the country's finances have to be managed.

While Bills, if passed, become part of the laws of the province, there is another method by which the will of the Assembly can be made known. Both Government and other members have the right to introduce 'Resolutions', which are also debated and discussed. A Resolution calls for some special form of Government action, such as the opening of a new college, the building of new roads, or the digging of canals in certain places. It does not make a new law or change an old law; it merely states what should, in the opinion of the House, be done by the Government. Resolutions are convenient, therefore, for urging special benefits and for solving single problems.

Since the actual work of Government has to be done in detail by a very large number of paid officials of all grades, Assembly members are given opportunities to show that they are watching how the task of administration is carried on. They have the right to ask questions in the Assembly. There is, in fact, a special hour set aside for questions on each day that the Assembly is in session. There is no limit to the kind of subject. Members ask scores of questions on all kinds of things, and the Government is usually obliged to give an answer or explanation. Thus, questions may be asked about an order given in a particular school, or the lectures in a college, or why certain roads are closed, or how many workers are employed on certain construction work or the wages they are paid. There is nothing of public interest which cannot be the subject of Assembly questions, which help to keep the public well informed about all kinds of matters and to prevent wrongful actions.

One of the most important duties of an Assembly is to decide about the money affairs of a province. Government has to spend money on a great number of things. It has to pay salaries, build roads, provide hospitals, support schools and colleges, buy seeds or machinery. The money comes mostly in the form of taxes paid by the citizens. All this cannot be left to chance or to the will of a few persons. The Assembly has the duty of seeing that proper accounts are kept by the Government, and that accurate estimates are made, both as to income and expenditure. It is the Assembly that controls the public purse, and it does this through the Budget and the Finance Bill.

The Budget has to be laid before the Assembly every year. It contains an exact statement of all the sums received by the Government and all the sums spent, item by item, department by department. It also contains full estimates of income and expenditure for the new year.

The Finance Bill has also to be introduced each year. When passed, it gives the Government permission to levy taxation only for twelve months and to spend the money only as agreed by the House. Every Finance Act is in fact a law lasting for only one year. In this way the Cabinet has to put all its accounts before the Assembly at least once a year, and there is no possibility of the people's money being collected or spent illegally. In ancient days, kings or emperors would issue personal orders to levy whatever taxes they pleased, and could spend the money just as they fancied. In a democracy the people's representatives keep a strict watch on the people's money and see that it is spent on things that benefit the public.

By long usage, the provinces obtain their income chiefly from land taxes, the sale of irrigation water, electricity charges, and rents. The Central (or Federal) Government, on the other hand, gets its revenue mainly from Income Tax, Customs, Central Excise Duties, Corporation Tax, Sales Tax, and Salt Tax. The Provincial Governments spend most of their money on what are known as the 'nation-building' departments. The Central (Federal) Government is responsible for Defence, Railways, and Posts and Telegraphs, and for big new development schemes.

For at any rate the time being the Federal Assembly is not elected directly by the people of Pakistan, but indirectly by the Provincial Assemblies. Its business is to make the nation's laws, and manage the great affairs of the country as a whole, leaving the provinces to attend to their own provincial interests. The Central Government has its own annual Budget and Finance Bill. It is always ready to help any province when special need arises.

Thanks to the great care and skill of our Central and

AN ASSEMBLY AT WORK 45

Provincial Assemblies and Governments, Pakistan has overcome many serious problems and difficulties in the first three years of its existence, and our country as a whole is well on the way to prosperity. When we grow old enough to become voters, we shall be able to help in electing the best representatives, and thus play our full part in promoting our country's welfare. Ours is a democracy—a land where we are governed with our own consent. Sovereignty (the right to rule) is ours; we exercise it through the ballot box. When we vote we do not create any masters over us; we merely, for the sake of convenience, pass the power for the time being into the hands of Assembly representatives whom we choose of our own free will. They are always responsible to us for the way they use that power.

CHAPTER VII

OUR DEFENCE FORCES

For a country to be happy and prosperous it is not enough that it should be wisely governed within its own boundaries. Trade, industry, education, and progress depend not only on internal contentment, but on the feeling that the country is safe from any external foe. Such a sense of security is just as necessary to-day as in the past.

We have many treasures to guard in our land of Pakistan—not only our material wealth, but our religion, our way of life, our culture, and our freedom. These cannot be protected only by words. We must be ready to fight against anyone who would try to take these precious things away from us.

Each of us piously hopes that war will never visit our happy land. War is an ugly and hateful thing. It destroys everything that is beautiful and sacred. Homes, crops, health, happiness, and liberty are all laid in ruins. We know how many countries suffered in the great World Wars of 1914–18 and 1939–45, and how they have not yet recovered from all the harmful results. Even to-day there are still some nations that are not satisfied with what they have, but seek to conquer other lands. They raise big armies, navies, and air forces, and constantly threaten their neighbours.

It is true that in some cases they are not successful. The United Nations Organization is ready to defend

OUR DEFENCE FORCES

smaller countries against stronger nations which invade them. It is necessary, however, that each peaceful country should be able and willing to help in its own defence and, if required, help to save others from invasion.

In the case of Pakistan we know full well that we do not wish to disturb the peace of any other country. We are satisfied with what we have or with what we rightly look upon as our own. We do not want to send our armies out to conquer other lands. All we desire is peace, so that we can cultivate our fields, make our own goods, and carry on trade safely with all the countries of the world. We also know, however, that we must be ready at all times to defend ourselves against causeless attacks by any possible enemy.

Fortunately, Pakistanis are a brave and united people, who love their country, and are willing to fight and, if need be, to die for it. All through history it has produced the finest of soldiers. There were many heroic figures among them who served the Moghals and the British with great honour and distinction. To-day we feel that we can depend upon every young Pakistani to serve his country, for the blood of warriors is in our veins even though we desire only peace.

It is, of course, not sufficient that a nation should trust to chance in such matters. Our statesmen try their best to keep our country friendly with others; but it makes their task easier if they know that the defence of our country is properly arranged. For this reason, even in times of peace, it is necessary in the world of to-day that we should have special armed forces ready to repel an enemy, and properly armed to do so. We have seen very recently how certain states have been siezed by invaders because their armed forces were too weak to offer much resistance.

Although we are not at present at war with any other countries, we should understand that we are surrounded by nations whose objects may not be all peaceful. We wish to make sure that there can be no danger to us from any of our neighbours. Afghanistan, Soviet Russia, China, Burma, and the Indian Republic are all rising countries. They have undergone many changes and we cannot foretell the future. If we want to be left in peace, we must see to it that we are strong enough to defend ourselves. A weak and helpless land is always a temptation to others.

War to-day is very much a scientific business. In ancient times, when warriors depended upon simple weapons, the population could take up arms at short notice and soon have sufficiently strong armies. Modern warfare, however, is quite different. Battles are fought with complicated weapons, and soldiers, sailors, and airmen have to undergo long and careful preparation. Defence has to be built up so as to protect land frontiers, sea frontiers, and the air above us. All kinds of scientific instruments have to be used, and our armed forces require a great deal of special equipment and training.

The defence of a country is best prepared by having a proper standing Army, Air Force, and Navy, whose members serve for long enough to receive full training. If war unfortunately breaks out, they are ready at once to fight. They are the 'first line of defence'. It is also necessary that every able-bodied man should have some training, so that in times of need he can be called upon to take up arms and serve. In some countries, while there are permanent soldiers, sailors, and airmen, the law compels every able-bodied young man to serve in the Forces for one or two years. This is known as 'conscription'. The United Kingdom has both a standing defence force and conscription, with a large reserve force known as the 'Territorial Army'.

In Pakistan we have no 'conscription'. We have only a standing Army, Navy, and Air Force, which any fit person can join for a fixed length of time of his own free will. There are also various military colleges and courses at which young Pakistani boys can be trained for future service. In addition, there is the Pakistan National Guard, in which ordinary civilians can be taught to drill and to handle arms, so that they can be of use to the country in times of emergency.

All our Armed Forces are in the charge of the Prime Minister, who is also Defence Minister. There are Commanders-in-Chief of each branch—the Army, the Navy, and the Air Force. Nearly all the officers are Pakistanis. For the first two or three years many hundreds of British officers helped to teach and train them and to organize the Forces properly. Some are still working with us. We are grateful to them for their co-operation. It is but natural, however, that we should wish to have only Pakistanis in our Forces, and the day is near when we shall depend entirely on our own nationals. Our Army Commander-in-Chief is a Pakistani.

Before examining each branch of our Defence Forces we should understand that they are part of the Army, Navy, and Air Force which were employed under British rule before the 1947 Partition. When the Indian continent was divided into the Dominion of Pakistan and the Republic of Bharat, the Armed Forces and their equipment were also divided between the two. Unfortunately, in the old 'Indian Army' there were no purely Muslim battalions, and it took some time to rearrange our men into suitable units. Much of our share of the weapons and general equipment lay scattered all over Bharat, and it proved difficult to collect the various items and bring them to Pakistan. Some never reached us. In our part of the continent also we did not at that time possess a single proper factory for military purposes.

Even in the short time since Partition, however, a vast improvement has taken place. Our Defence Forces are now well organized. Ordnance factories, where guns, rifles, ammunition, tanks, armoured cars, and other equipment can be made, are already working, and others are being built. We now have repair shops where work can be quickly carried out on our aeroplanes and armoured cars. We have also been able to buy much machinery and defence equipment from Britain and other countries. The result is that our Forces are now well arranged, well supplied, and well trained. No invader can afford to despise them.

Pakistan's Army to-day is not very large, but it is well organized, and all branches are complete. Besides infantry, it consists of artillery and armoured regiments, with the necessary supply, transport, medical, and engineering units. The senior officers and commanders are trained at the Staff College, Quetta, where they have the advantage of meeting great British, Canadian, and Australian soldiers who also come to study there. Some of our senior officers also go to study at the Staff College, Camberley, in England, and at staff colleges in Australia and Canada.

Our younger officers are trained chiefly at the Pakistan Military Academy at Jhelum, and the special Officers' Training School at Kohat, and at King George's Royal

Pakistan Military College at Kakul, which teach them all the arts of war and of leadership. There are also the Pakistan Army School of Education at Lower Topa (near Murree), the Pakistan Infantry School, the School of Military Engineering, and several other institutions of that kind. Very many of our young officers and cadets are also sent to receive training in England, where they are much admired as good fellows and good sportsmen. There are splendid regimental training centres as well in Pakistan for older boys who may wish to join the Army.

Although our country has only short sea frontiers, in both East and West Pakistan, there are important ports and harbours which have to be protected. In the west there is Karachi, with its immensely large export and import trade with Europe, the Middle East, and Africa, and the west coast of India. From there go our shiploads of cotton, timber, hides and skins, oilseeds, minerals, and other merchandise to Aden, Basra, Bombay, Surat, Zanzibar, Suez, and the Western World. Into Karachi come the coal, steel, piece-goods, machinery, and other imports which we need. In the east we have our nearly equally great port of Chittagong, whose trade with Burma, Malaya, China, the East Indies, and Australia is increasing enormously. From Chittagong we send our jute, rice, tea, linseed, and much other valuable produce, while ships from abroad bring coal, machinery, cloth, and other necessaries. The construction of another large port at Chalna, not far from Chittagong, is also just beginning.

The Navy has not only to guard these great seaports, but to protect the ships which use them. It must be ready to lay mines and anti-submarine defences, and to escort merchant vessels to and from both Karachi and Chittagong. It must also act as the 'policeman' of our sea coasts and our navigable rivers and guard against unexpected attacks by pirates. Although pirates have long been put down, they were at one time plentiful at the mouths of the Megna River at Chittagong, while Arab pirates used to be a nuisance off the Sind coast in ages long past. Ships in distress during cyclones may also be in need of help, and this can best be given by the skilful sailors of our Navy.

Pakistan has at present only a small fleet. Some of our vessels were handed over to us at the 1947 Partition, and others have since been obtained from Britain. The ships have been renamed. Most famous among them are the destroyers *Sind* and *Shamsher*. Although not big battleships, they are very suitable for our purposes. There are also several smaller frigates. Altogether the Pakistan Navy has at least eight big ships and eight small craft, including mine-sweepers. All these have been refitted and brought completely up-to-date at naval dockyards in England, and are powerful fighting units.

Our country has always had brave and strong seamen, who in past ages were noted, not only as fishermen, but as mariners and navigators. Thousands annually sailed the seas in the service of British-owned passenger liners and cargo vessels. When the 1947 Partition took place, 180 Muslim officers and 3,400 Muslim ratings came over to Pakistan from the old Royal Indian Navy. In addition, sufficient numbers were easy to find at both Karachi and Chittagong. There were also some officers of the Naval Volunteer Reserve.

A great deal has been done since the founding of our country to make the Pakistan Navy a really smart and efficient force. The cadets are obtained through a competitive examination held thrice a year by the Pakistan Public Service Commission, and are finally chosen only after interviews by a selection board. The cadets go through a short course of training at Karachi, and are then sent to the United Kingdom for three to five years, according to the branch for which they have been chosen. They are trained alongside the British cadets, at the Royal Naval College, Dartmouth, where many of our lads have earned distinctions. We are thus sure of a good supply of our own Pakistani officers and men for this great branch of our national forces.

Besides training, the Pakistan Navy has been able to make arrangements to keep our ships in good fighting order. Pakistan will soon have its own naval dockyard, where repair work of all kinds can be carried out. Our training ships and depots are also being provided with modern machinery and instruments, so that full instruction can be given to our cadets here.

Ours is by no means a 'stay-at-home' Navy. Our ships have more than once taken part in sea exercises and manoeuvres with ships of the British and United States navies. They have shown that they can shoot well and take part in dropping depth-charges and other anti-submarine operations. Our sailors have also earned good fame as sportsmen, both here and in Britain.

Just as important as the Army and the Navy is our third fighting service, the Pakistan Air Force. 'A country without a strong Air Force is at the mercy of any aggressor', said the Quaid-i-Azam. 'Pakistan must build up her Air Force as quickly as possible. It must take its right place in securing Pakistan's defence.'

Our country has paid good heed to our noble Founder's advice, and very great progress has been made in creating a strong and efficient Air Force. Full attention is being given to providing both men and machines. These two have to be of the highest quality. Modern aeroplanes are very complicated structures, fitted with innumerable scientific devices. They have to be perfect machines and must be kept in perfect condition. Our airmen too need to be highly educated and fully trained, with a proper sense of daring, responsibility, and readiness, able to make quick decisions and thoroughly fit in body and mind.

Both officers and men are chosen very carefully by the Air Selection Board at Lahore, and by Air Selection Centres at Karachi, Lahore, Rawalpindi, and Dacca. Only the best are accepted. Their training is done mostly in Pakistan. At Risalpur we have our splendid Pakistan Air Force College, where all cadets in all branches of pilot training are taught their difficult profession. These cadets will be the future permanent officers, who in turn will train others for the Pakistan Air Force. The course is a very wide one, and includes many sciences besides actual flying. A cadet has to learn much about mathematics, aerodynamics, airmanship, navigation, service customs, history, and geography. Besides ground training he has to be taught simple flying and then more advanced work, such as bombing exercises, air to ground firing, and ciné-camera operation; finally, formation flying, armament, gunnery, and combat. It takes two full years for the successful cadet to gain the much-prized cream-white wings of the P.A.F.

Annually six cadets go to England for training at the R.A.F. College, Cranwell. Several senior Pakistani officers also go each year to the R.A.F. Staff College at Andover, England. Special cadets are sometimes sent to the United States; many Pakistani pilots, navigators, and signallers attend the central flying and gunnery schools in the United Kingdom. We also have centres of our own —at Kohat and at Drigh Road (near Karachi), where large numbers of aircraftmen are trained. We further send forty apprentices every year to the R.A.F. Technical Training School at Halton (in the U.K.).

While every care is thus taken to train our airmen and ground crews thoroughly, our Government has also given our Air Force the most modern of aircraft. Fighter planes, bombers, and transport planes are to-day of suitable kinds. To keep them in perfect running order we have the latest workshops, signals, and radar equipment. Our aerodromes are also kept in the best condition.

With many gallant deeds already to its credit, especially during the air operations in Azad Kashmir, the P.A.F. offers a splendid career to any keen, sporting, and intelligent young Pakistani. It is a worthy branch of our Defence Forces, and, if we are attacked, it will play a vital part in defeating our enemies.

CHAPTER VIII

THE FACTORS OF PRODUCTION

OUR country is already known as a great one. It can soon take its place among the leading countries of the world. So long as we all make up our minds to help in every possible way, steady progress can be made in all directions. It is necessary for us to understand, however, that a great many things remain to be done before Pakistan becomes as highly civilized and prosperous as we would all wish to see it. In many parts of the country our people are still very poor, and large numbers still do not know how to read or write. Also many have not yet learned how to make full use of their talents and their opportunities.

All the same, Pakistan begins with many things in its favour. First of all, not only is the soil very fertile in most of the districts, but in various parts there is great mineral wealth under the soil. Secondly, our people themselves are intelligent, hard-working and, as a rule, strong and naturally healthy. Thirdly, we are learning to use our money properly, and the goods that we sell to other countries bring our nation more money with which to improve our fields, our mines, and our factories.

Wherever enough water can be obtained, the soil of Pakistan produces good crops of wheat, rice, cotton, jute, tea, sugar-cane, timber, fruit, and fodder. It supports millions of cattle, sheep, goats, camels, and horses. In addition, there are all kinds of valuable minerals lying

THE FACTORS OF PRODUCTION 57

far under our feet—such as petroleum, coal, limestone, rock salt, chromite, gypsum, sulphur, antimony, and clay.

The surface of the country too is of a helpful kind. Although there are mighty mountain ranges on some of its frontiers, Pakistan (both East and West) consists mostly of level plains through which big rivers flow. The rivers not only bring water for our fields, but allow us to use boats and steamers to carry passengers and goods. The Indus, for example, is navigable for several hundred miles from near Attock to the sea. Small boats and steam launches can also use many portions of the 'five rivers' (Jhelum, Chenab, Ravi, Beas, and Sutlej). The flatness of the land has made easy the building of canals, which bring water to the dry districts (though very few of the canals are used by boats). In Eastern Pakistan the great mouths of the Ganges and Brahmaputra Rivers provide us with a network of thousands of miles of waterways, where large numbers of barges and river steamers are always busy carrying rich cargoes.

So far as climate is concerned, East and West Pakistan differ strangely from each other; but in each case the climate is helpful, even if it does create some difficulties. In Western Pakistan, where the heat is very great in summer and the cold intense in winter, with only a small amount of monsoon rainfall, the climate is very suitable for the growing of wheat, maize, oilseeds, barley, gram, jowar and cotton, fruit, and sugar-cane. In Eastern Pakistan, the annual rainfall is far heavier, and extremes of heat and cold are not so common; the climate there is more favourable to the growing of rice, tea and jute, gram, oilseeds, betel leaves, plantains, sugar-cane, and tobacco.

When the seasons are good and the rainfall neither too

heavy nor too light, the immensely fertile soil of both East and West Pakistan brings forth splendid harvests, which mean prosperity to all. Even in the so-called 'deserts' of Western Pakistan, we know that the soil is extremely fertile, and that rich crops can be grown there as soon as canals are constructed. In course of time we can expect to see far bigger and better crops raised all over East and West Pakistan, and stronger and more useful animals bred.

Nature has in fact not been too unkind to our country. Our land is full of natural resources and we are glad to think also that our people have a splendid name as workers. Provided we are able to guard their health and free them from diseases like plague, cholera, smallpox, typhoid fever, malaria, kala-azar, and beriberi (the last two being far more common in the East than in the West), Pakistanis do extremely well both in agriculture and in industry. They are hardy and strong. They can work long hours in field or factory. Their sight is generally keen, and they are highly skilled in all kinds of handwork. Many become expert mechanics, and quickly learn modern methods of producing goods.

The second important factor of production, 'Labour', is therefore plentiful in Pakistan. The people are ready and willing to work, and they have long proved their worth. What is needed is to teach them still better methods of agriculture or industry and to provide them with better seeds, better livestock, better tools, and better machinery. The clumsy and heavy implements of past ages are not good enough for the needs of to-day. We know, for example, that wheat grown from good seed fetches a bigger price; so too with cotton, jute, and everything else. The farmer who is wise enough to grow

THE FACTORS OF PRODUCTION 59

long-staple American cotton obtains a bigger reward for his trouble than does one who grows only short-staple *desi* cotton. Similarly, the zemindar or ryot who ploughs his land with the help of modern machinery such as a tractor, has less trouble and expense than one who uses only the old-fashioned ploughshare drawn by bullocks. Our Government is eager to supply cultivators with improved seed and with machinery. In time we hope to see grand crops in all our fields, which will mean far happier lives for our peasantry. There is no reason why they should not become some day as prosperous as the farmers of the United States, Australia, New Zealand, or Britain.

In the same way, our industrial workers also need a great deal of help and training. The making of goods in Pakistan is carried on in two ways—in the homes of the people, and in factories. The man who works only with his hands cannot compare with the man who knows how to use machinery. Our cottage industries, such as spinning and weaving, woodwork, metalwork, and leatherwork, are still very largely carried on by hand. To-day, however, the Government are doing their best to teach cottage workers how to use simple machinery, and are making it easier for them to buy or hire such machinery. Electricity is now obtainable in many places, and at such a cheap price as to bring it within the reach of the poorer workers. Machinery enables them to make far more goods in the same time and to give their articles a better finish, as compared with ordinary handwork.

Even if our people grow better crops and make more goods, it is necessary to help the producers to sell them at the best prices. There are, of course, the usual marketplaces and *melas,* where buyers and sellers can make their own bargains. The Government, however, are anxious to help in many other ways. Both zemindar and manufacturer need sums of money for the purchase of their seeds, raw materials, machinery, buildings, and other necessary expenses. The Government are doing their best to offer loans at a very low rate of repayment, and are also encouraging the banks, co-operative societies, and rich people to lend money to the people in this way.

This money side of any business is different from the two other 'factors of production' to which we have already given the names of 'Land' and 'Labour'. In fact, nevertheless, it is just as important. 'Land' and 'Labour' are of little use without 'Capital'. There must be sums of money ready in the form of savings or loans, with which to carry on the real business of farm, cottage industry, or factory. Money is necessary for the purchase of seeds, raw materials, and machinery; for the building of work places and storage godowns; for the carriage of products to markets or to far-off towns. In the case of bigger factories, money is also needed for paying wages, for the keeping of accounts, for advertising, and for other expenses.

In Pakistan, as in most other countries of the world, our 'business capital' consists chiefly of the money saved and set aside by the people themselves, and also of the profit made from things which we sell to other countries. Even when capital takes the form of loans granted by the Government, the money has really come from the taxes which we pay. We have all, therefore, to try to add to the capital wealth of Pakistan by making and selling more things to other nations, by avoiding waste of wealth in any form, and by putting our money and brains to the most fruitful use.

These three 'factors of production'—Land, Labour,

THE FACTORS OF PRODUCTION 61

and Capital—all depend on each other, like the three legs of a stool. If you remove one, the two others cannot stand alone. Without **Land** in the form of fields or mines or forests the labourer would be unable to work, and there would be no return for any capital invested. Or without **Labour** there could be no work done in field, mine, forest, or factory. And without **Capital** it would be impossible nowadays to have any proper business arranged.

Every young Pakistani citizen will some day have a part to play in his country's future. He may be connected in some way with agriculture or with industry; or he may hold some position in a bank, a Government office, a shop, or some other business. Whatever he does is sure to have some effect upon the country's welfare. If he owns fields or mines, he will try to put them to the best use; if he has a factory, he will introduce the most useful machines, train his workmen, and produce valuable goods. If he is a Government official, he will seek to make the best arrangements for his fellow-countrymen. Even if he is to be only a cultivator, or a factory labourer, a railwayman or a shopkeeper, he can by his honest efforts help to make Pakistan more and more prosperous. If he has riches, he can take a big share in promoting schemes which add to his country's wealth. Whatever his lot in life, he has it in his power to provide Land, Labour, or Capital. The sum of such efforts by her eighty million sons and daughters will make sure of a safe and happy future for our Pakistan.

CHAPTER IX

LIFE IN OUR VILLAGES

PAKISTAN is still a long way from becoming a country of manufacturers. It is true that we all wish to see more industries created, so that there can be enough work at all times for those Pakistanis who have no land of their own or who have not been accustomed to growing crops. We have to remember, too, that many of the Muslim refugees who fled from Bharat at the time of the 1947 Partition came from manufacturing towns and cities like Amritsar, Ludhiana, Delhi, Cawnpore, Agra, and many places in Bombay Presidency. (There were, however, many Muslim ryots also from the Eastern Punjab and the United Provinces, and many of these have been given land so that they can again cultivate fields.)

For many centuries the chief occupation of the people of Pakistan has been agriculture. Only here and there in more modern times did they have an opportunity to learn other trades. The railway workshops at Moghalpura gave employment to thousands of skilled or partly skilled artisans, such as carpenters, machine operators, foundrymen, mechanics, and electricians. A number of cotton ginning factories also sprang up before the Partition, while motor-car repair shops and motor-bus depots also provided work. In the cities there has always been a big demand for builders' labourers, while dock-hands and sailors found work at the seaports. In a later chapter we shall learn more about the growth of industries.

LIFE IN OUR VILLAGES

The chief concern of our people, in both Western and Eastern Pakistan, has been to grow food or other crops. The result is that we are a nation of village-dwellers, scattered all over the districts. Our villages contain on an average between 500 and 2,000 inhabitants, whose only interest is the welfare of their fields. Usually they know very little about anything outside their own small group of villages. They rarely enter a large town, though they often go to the shops in their nearest market town, where they sell their grain, their jute, or their cotton, and buy their cloth.

As a result of having so little to do with the outside world our villagers are very simple people, most of whom receive next to no education. Even if they were once sent to school, many of them were still so young when they left school that they have forgotten how to read or write. Although they may know a fair amount about the growing of crops, they remain ignorant about the progress taking place around them. The farmer does not like to change his old-fashioned ways. Only too often he thinks that what was good enough for his grandfathers is still good enough for himself.

Village life in Eastern and Western Pakistan has therefore made only a small amount of real progress during the past fifty years. In some ways this has been a good thing, for the villager is so closely connected with the lives of his neighbours that he feels he really belongs to a community. He is also happy and contented with his simple home and his daily life. Perhaps he is too easily satisfied and does not sufficiently feel any cause to improve his standard of living. As compared with villagers of other countries, he does not always get enough to eat, and his earnings are too small for him to build a better house for his family or wear better clothes. He has no luxuries. Except for rare pilgrimages, he knows nothing about the outer world.

Although differences in climate make the villages of Western Pakistan look very unlike those of Eastern Pakistan, the kind of life led in the two regions is almost identical. In the West Punjab and Sind the ryot builds himself a mud hut with a flat roof. Brick houses are now more numerous than in the old days, but they are not as cool in summer, nor so warm in winter. In the North-West Frontier Province the peasants make much use of stone cemented with mud, the roof being of rough slate; or the walls may be made of mud mixed with straw, while wooden beams support the flat mud roof.

In Eastern Bengal the houses are generally built of bamboo, even the walls and roofs being of that material. They stand on a platform of baked mud. Each house has its own small patch of land, planted with fruit trees and palm trees, and surrounded with a fence.

As all the villagers are closely related and well known to each other, they form very democratic groups, and are mostly left to manage their village affairs by themselves without outside interference. Their disputes, which are often about the boundaries or water or damage to crops, are settled by the village *panchayat*, which is an assembly of the local elders. They have a headman who attends to much of the official business and who is always an influential person. The larger villages have their own school, post office, police station, and dispensary. These are also provided for groups of small villages.

Pakistani villagers have from ancient times been able to supply almost all their own needs. This has helped to keep them cut off from the outside world. They grow enough food of all kinds for their daily meals. In addition, there is usually a village cobbler, a village weaver, a village blacksmith (*lohar*), a potter, and a carpenter, these trades being handed down from father to son. Men and women take an equal share of work in the fields, and even small children do lighter jobs, such as tending sheep and cattle. Some of the people take up cattle-raising, horse-breeding, or sheep-rearing. Although each family looks after its own fields, at sowing-time or harvest-time they all help each other, taking a share in common tasks.

Although at first glance it may be thought that our villagers are happy and contented, we must not shut our eyes to certain important defects in our rural life. Nearly nine out of ten Pakistanis live in the villages and work on the land. They thus form by far the biggest portion of our population, and their needs have to be our biggest care. We cannot feel satisfied with conditions as they are, and we must all do our best to improve the village folks' lot, since they form the bulk of the population.

Our ryots are far too dependent on the climate and the seasons. A good monsoon may bring splendid crops, but when bad times come the cultivators have no other ways of making up their loss of earnings. Too many of them know only how to grow food or raise livestock. When the monsoon is weak and rainfall insufficient, they are quickly in want and distress. It would be different if more of them knew how to make useful things for sale outside their villages. Even in good seasons they are not working all the year round in the fields; they have weeks of leisure, when their crops do not need so much attention. At present they do not know what to do with their spare time. If more of them were taught various cottage industries, such as spinning and weaving, rope-making, woodwork, and metalwork—or embroidery and lace-making for the women and girls—they would be able to earn extra money, and would have some way of making a living in times of bad harvests.

Health conditions are also in need of improvement in the country. Although the villagers keep their own bodies clean and their houses are generally spotless, they have not been taught sufficiently in the past how to prevent outbreaks of epidemic disease. In Western Pakistan plague kills thousands annually because the villagers still have the custom of storing their grain inside their houses. When the harvesting is done and there is no food left in the fields, the rats follow the grain into the homes of the people. If those rats are infected with plague-carrying fleas, an epidemic of this dangerous disease can easily break out and cause many deaths. This could be avoided by encouraging the ryots to construct grain storage bins or godowns some distance away from their houses. Rat-proof godowns are very necessary in the towns. Rats should not be allowed to breed anywhere and should be destroyed. Apart from the loss of life they cause through plague, they eat our grain and damage our property.

Cholera also plays havoc in many parts of Pakistan. The cholera germ is carried far and wide by flies. Our villagers should be shown how to get together and destroy the swarms of flies which blacken the roads and which pollute their food. They should also learn how to remove any heaps of dirt and prevent refuse from being thrown into the streets and roads, and thus prevent the flies from having so many easy breeding-places.

Malaria, too, causes severe loss of life and weakens our people. It is caused by the bite of the anopheles mosquito (the striped mosquito which 'stands on its head' when it feeds on a person's blood) which pours the malaria germ into our veins. By joint action it is fairly easy to prevent mosquitoes from breeding in pools, water channels, and drains.

The three principal diseases which we have just mentioned are spread through the sheer ignorance or carelessness of our peasants. Epidemics could be completely stamped out, if only the people could be made to understand the simple facts about public sanitation. They are clean in their personal habits. They must be taught also that this is not enough, but that there are certain acts of neglect or certain harmful practices which affect the general welfare in town and village alike.

A proper understanding of such matters can come only through the spread of education. There are not enough schools in Pakistan's villages. The people should be encouraged to open more schools everywhere. In the whole of our country fewer than half the number of boys of school-going age are actually attending school, and only one girl in every ten. Our Government are eager to provide more schools. We should make up our minds to help in this great work, and especially to tell the ryots how important it is that their children should be taught. In school they learn not only to read and write and to do sums, but about how to lead healthy lives and to prevent sickness. The children who are taught this will be more careful to keep their towns and villages clean and healthy. In many other countries of the world—all the countries of Europe, North America, Australia, and South Africa —all children between the ages of 5 and 14 go to school, and their parents are punished if they do not send them.

When every boy and girl in Pakistan receives a proper education, they will learn that many other improvements can be carried out in our villages. They will understand, for example, that they can obtain better results through the use of machinery and of manures on the land. They will want to replace the slow and clumsy bullock cart with power-driven vans and lorries; they will see the need for building better roads to replace the *kachcha* roads which now link the villages with the market towns.

Our educated boys and girls will thus grow up to be intelligent and enterprising men and women, able to lead fuller and happier lives. Their leisure will be better spent and their minds and bodies improved by healthy recreation. All the wonderful inventions of modern science are ready to serve them.

Other countries have gained a long start over us. Yet we should remember that only 150 years ago the land labourers of a country like England were very poor and uneducated. Few then knew how to read or write, and their earnings were extremely small. After 1870 came a great and wonderful change. It became the law of England that every boy and girl must go to school. This meant that the poorest children could learn all kinds of useful knowledge. As England progressed, the villages became happier and better places, with more comfortable houses and many other improvements. Machinery took the place of hand work on the farms as well as in the factories. The whole life of the country became healthier and more prosperous.

A village in England to-day remains beautiful, and in some cases the homes of the people are provided with electricity, water pipes, and underground drainage. Splendid roads lead to the towns. On the farms the ploughing, sowing, and harvesting are done by wonderful machines. Even the cows are milked by electricity. There are fine schools, and the poorest children have a chance to go to college. All are well fed and well clothed. They are looked after free of charge by the Government's own doctors and dentists. There are free hospitals for cases of illness or accident. In nearly every village home there is a wireless set, and some of the peasants have their own television receivers. Their village halls hold entertainments of all kinds, and the village sports clubs provide opportunities for football, cricket, and other outdoor recreations.

It should not be thought that in England all this has been a sudden recent change. The improvements in Western life have come about gradually. They would not have been possible without education for all. So also in Pakistan we need not expect a miracle, but we can as surely expect a steady improvement in the lives of all our people if we open the way by giving all our boys and girls an education. When that is done, our villages will be grand places to live in, and our peasants will be as prosperous as our townsfolk.

CHAPTER X

WATER MEANS WEALTH

To few countries in the world does water mean more than it does to Pakistan. Both in East and West it is the chief thing upon which the prosperity and well-being of our people depend. It is still too true to say that a good monsoon makes all the difference. In years to come, however, we may see some very great improvements in the control of our water resources. This, of course, does not mean that we human beings can cause good or bad seasons of rainfall; what is meant is that by great engineering schemes we can bring about better use of the water which a bountiful Providence bestows.

There is a great difference between Eastern and Western Pakistan in regard to the supply of water for our fields. Eastern Bengal districts have a very abundant monsoon rainfall—sometimes too abundant. It is on an average thrice as heavy in Eastern Bengal as in Western Pakistan. In some cases the difference is still greater. In the Dacca district, for example, the annual rainfall averages 70 inches; in Sind and Baluchistan as a whole the average annual rainfall is less than 8 inches. When the great Brahmaputra River rises in flood, large parts of Eastern Bengal are left under water, and crops cannot be grown until the low-lying lands are drained.

The total area of Pakistan is 200 million acres. We grow crops on only 45 million acres. Thus, 155 million acres are still uncultivated, though much of this area could be used for crops. We should notice, however, that we have about 8 million acres of purely forest land. Only 32 million acres of our country are barren mountain regions unfit for cultivation.

In 30 million of the 45 million cultivated acres, we rely upon artificial methods of supplying water. In the remaining 15 million acres the natural rainfall is ordinarily good enough. Roughly speaking, if water could be obtained in proper quantities, there are in the whole of Pakistan at least 105 million acres now idle, on which we could grow more grain and more cotton as well as other crops. Most of this usable land is in Western Pakistan.

In ancient times, during the period of the Indus Valley civilization, it appears probable that Sind and the Western Punjab had a heavier annual rainfall than now. This is shown by the fact that the inhabitants there 3,500 years ago used millions of baked bricks for their houses. Baked bricks are preferable to unbaked mud bricks, because they are more suitable for a rainy climate. There must have been big forests to supply the firewood used for the baking of those bricks, and such forests require good rainfall. Also the ancient drawings which we have discovered in those parts are of tigers, water-buffaloes, elephants, and rhinoceroses, which flourish only in a rainy country.

Later, perhaps on account of wars which destroyed the forests and the crops, the land slowly changed into semi-desert country and the soil became poorer because the rainfall had decreased as a natural consequence of the disappearance of vegetation.

There are three ways in which a supply of water can be obtained for irrigation in dry regions, namely, wells, storage tanks, and canals leading from the rivers. There have always been wells in Western Pakistan, and they are a familiar sight everywhere. Unfortunately, there are never enough wells, and a well after all can supply water to only a rather small field. Open storage tanks are not very suitable in such a hot and dry climate as ours, because evaporation is so great, and it is impossible to prevent much of the water from being lost through that cause. Canals are perhaps the best method, especially underground canals such as we commonly find at the foot of the mountains (even in the frontier districts there are many examples of covered water-channels).

Canals are of three kinds, according to the way in which they derive their water. The simplest are 'inundation' canals, which are water-channels (artificial or semi-artificial) unprovided with any means of regulating or controlling the supply at the point where they leave the river; they are filled only when the river rises in flood, and are quite dry when the river level is low.

Secondly, there are 'periodic' canals, which obtain their water from rivers having a changeable and uncertain supply. In order to prevent the water running to waste, some kind of temporary or permanent dam is built across the river-bed to hold, store up, and lead aside the water into the canal either during the rainy season, or when the river level is high enough.

Thirdly, we have 'perennial' canals, which draw their supply from rivers having a sufficient volume of water at all times of the year, without previous storage. Such canals are equipped with dams or weirs and other 'head works' for raising and regulating the supply of water according to requirements.

The earliest canals in Pakistan were built before the Moghals came, and traces of them can still be seen. By the time of the Moghal invasion it is clear that many parts of Western Pakistan had become very dry and the deserts had spread far and wide.

The Moghal emperors were great lovers of water and of the coolness which it gave to their palaces. They were fond of building pleasure houses surrounded with large gardens. As gardens must have plenty of water, the Moghals and their nobles constructed canals from the rivers. The beautiful Shalimar Garden at Lahore is a famous example. Its water was brought to it by a channel (dating from about 1640) from the Ravi River, and this channel later became part of the modern Bari Doab Canal. The Moghals made much use of the older inundation canals, some of which were fairly large. In the great plain below the junction of the five rivers there were pre-Moghal canals varying from 10 to 300 feet in width, from 8 to 10 feet in depth, and of all lengths up to 60 or 70 miles. Later the British cleared and improved these channels and by degrees constructed very many more.

The first important irrigation work carried out by the British Government in India was the restoration (in 1817–20) of Shah Jehan's old Delhi branch canal (which, however, is now in Bharat). It was in 1849 that a plan for irrigating the waterless districts lying between the Ravi and Beas Rivers was taken up by the British Government. Here, in the region known as the Bari Doab, there had remained the old 'Husli Canal' first built by the Emperor Shah Jehan for his royal gardens at Shalimar (as mentioned above). The British made it into a deeper, wider, and longer channel, and in 1873 completed a weir at the head of the canal on the Ravi at Madhopur, where the river leaves the Himalaya Mountains.

Since then very many more great canals have been

constructed in Western Pakistan. There is in fact no other country in the world with such a huge network of irrigation canals. All the five big rivers are connected with each other in this way, and their water is spilled over the fertile soil for many tens of thousands of square miles. Altogether our canals in Western Pakistan alone give abundant water to about 13½ million acres. They have made it possible for millions of cultivators to settle in new colonies. They have made sure that even in bad monsoons there is enough water for all to grow reasonably good crops. They have not only prevented famine in their own regions, but have allowed so much grain to be grown there that there has been some to spare for other places in times of scarcity. Although they cost very large sums of money for their construction, they have more than repaid the expense through the sale of water alone, and have brought enormous wealth to our country through the export of wheat, cotton, oilseeds, and other products.

The following are the principal irrigation canals in Western Pakistan:—

Name	Districts watered	Area irrigated (acres)
Upper Bari Doab	Lahore, etc.	1,200,000
Lower Chenab	Gujranwala, Lyallpur, and Jhang	3,330,000
* Upper Jhelum	Gujrat and Shahpur	350,000
* Upper Chenab	Gujranwala	650,000
* Lower Bari Doab	Montgomery and Multan	1,000,000
Lower Jhelum	Shahpur and Jhang	750,000
Lower Surat	Peshawar	170,000
Upper Surat	Peshawar and Malakand	382,000
Sukkur	Sind	6,000,000

(Four new projects planned—12,000,000 more acres)

* Triple Project

In addition to these existing canals, several new great irrigation works have been planned under the Pakistan Government and will add enormously to the area under cultivation. These are:

Name	Districts to benefit	Acres to be irrigated
Thal Project	Shahpur, and Mianwali	831,000
Lower Sind Barrage	Sind	2,000,000
Rasul Tube-well Project	N.W.F.P.	750,000
Mianwali	N.W.F.P.	
Upper Sind Barrage	Sind and Bahawalpur	140,000

Most of the many thousands of tube wells which will be used for the Rasul Project are being manufactured in Pakistan factories. In some cases these wells go deep into the earth, to reach unseen underground water which is then pumped to the surface by machinery. A tube well is usually made of long steel pipes joined together, only a few inches in diameter, and driven into the ground. It can supply many thousands of gallons of water every hour; in one day it can produce as much water as several ordinary wells of the Persian-wheel kind. A tube well can be worked by a small petrol engine.

So far we have dealt chiefly with irrigation in Western Pakistan, where the great need is to bring more water to the surface soil. The problem is a very different one in Eastern Pakistan, where in many areas there is too much water. The land, which is very flat there, is cut up by numerous large rivers and water channels. It has only a slight slope and after heavy rainfall or when the rivers overflow their banks Eastern Pakistan is liable to severe floods. The water sometimes does not flow away readily, but remains several feet deep in low-lying districts. The result often is that ploughing and sowing cannot be carried out at the proper season and in this way crops are lost and the ryots earn less money. The water stays too deep even for rice and jute crops, which ordinarily require a good deal of water.

Owing to the ground being so level and the flow of the rivers so slow even when in flood, the water channels and rivers become blocked with silt (mud brought down by the rivers). This mud sinks to the bottom and, although it makes the land very fertile, it is harmful in other ways. It makes whole districts permanently waterlogged, because the natural drainage becomes blocked with silt, and it also causes serious epidemics of malaria through creating numerous breeding-places for the anopheles mosquito.

Our engineers have therefore planned or already begun many large and small schemes to clear away the mud from the blocked water channels and *khals* or *bils* of Eastern Bengal. In some cases the rivers will also be deepened by dredging their beds so as to remove the silt. This will enable the water to flow away through the ordinary channels and will allow the soil to be cultivated again. When these schemes are completed, many more lakhs of maunds of rice and jute crops will be obtained in the districts concerned. The crores of rupees which are being spent on irrigation in Eastern Pakistan will thus be regained several times over through the money value of the bigger harvests which will result.

What has already been done in the first three years of our country's life is only a beginning. There is much more to be done in both East and West. Year by year we shall have to keep on making new canals and 're-claiming' waterlogged land. There are still 105 million acres which are waiting to be cultivated. Luckily our great rivers contain all the water we require, and by using scientific methods of engineering and control we need never fear a shortage. Every year will see more and more of the western deserts changed into smiling fields of wheat and cotton, while Eastern Bengal will gradually be freed of the fear of floods. Pakistan will again be one of the great 'granaries' of the world.

CHAPTER XI

THE SOIL AND ITS PROTECTION

EXCEPT in the mountain regions, the soil in Eastern and Western Pakistan is almost everywhere very suitable for crops. Mixed up with the sand and the clay on the surface is a good quantity of decayed leaves, grass, bark, twigs, and other organic matter. All these are in such tiny pieces that they can hardly be seen with the naked eye.

Yet we can sometimes separate them from the soil. If we place a lump of soil from our fields in a glass tumbler and mix it with water poured into the tumbler, we see nothing at first except a brown muddy liquid. After a few minutes, however, the sandy portion sinks to the bottom; near the top of the glass the water begins to get clearer, while below it is a cloudy brown layer. By degrees small particles of lighter substances float to the surface and other tiny pieces can also be seen just below the surface of the water. These are the remains of dead leaves, grass, and other 'organic' materials which have been mixed in the soil.

We have seen how leaves fall from the trees and wither and crumble into dust on the ground. We also know that grass and stalks of plants slowly decay. The dust into which they are turned is blown all over the surface of the land by the winds, and is thus scattered far and wide. When rain falls on the mountains and forests it carries big quantities of decayed organic matter into the streams

Top: Bamboo huts in an Eastern Pakistan village.
Below: Brick cottages of a neat and clean village in England.

Top: Bullocks slowly dragging a wooden plough.

Below: A tractor-drawn triple-share steel plough works twenty times as fast.

THE SOIL AND ITS PROTECTION

and rivers. When the rivers overflow or when their water is led into canals and spread over our fields, this organic matter becomes mixed with the soil.

Like ourselves, plants are living things. They need food, otherwise they cannot grow in size and in strength. Human beings and animals feed themselves through their mouths. Plants, trees, and grass feed themselves through their roots. Their food takes the form of the tiny pieces of decayed organic matter dissolved in the moisture contained in the soil. In addition to this organic matter the soil contains very small quantities of chemicals, such as ammonium sulphate, iron, potassium, and lime. Plants need these also as food. There is one more important fact which we must understand. Unless dissolved in water, no 'food' can enter the roots of a plant. That is why, before crops can grow, there must be some moisture in the soil. If the soil is completely dry, the plant starves, withers, and dies. Hence the need for our fields to be kept properly watered, whether by rain or by wells and canals.

The chemicals should also be in right quantities. Too much salt or saltpetre is harmful to many plants. That is why wheat, cotton, and other crops do not grow in some parts of Western Pakistan, where the saltpetre lies in big white patches on the surface of the land.

In our last chapter we showed how much has been done to bring water to our fields or to drain land where too much water collects. There are, however, other ways in which we have to look after the soil and keep it in the best condition so that it can continue to grow the finest of crops.

Until recent times the soil, especially in West Pakistan, was badly neglected by the people, because they had not learned to understand what elements it contained or what steps were necessary to preserve it. Even though science has taught us many things, there are still very many cultivators who remain in ignorance. Before learning about the various crops which we grow, we should thoroughly know how the soil should be treated and kept in its best condition.

Crops grow on the 'food' contained in the surface soil. If we dig a field, we find that the top layer is darker in colour and more easily broken up. When we dig deeper we come across only gravel or sand; go deeper still, and there is nothing but big stones or solid rock. The surface soil, which is the real crop-bearing layer, may be only a few inches in depth in some places. On an average it is about 25 inches deep in Western Pakistan, but in some areas it may be as deep as 8 or 10 feet.

If we remove that fertile outer covering of the earth, and try to grow crops in the sand or rock underneath, no seeds will germinate. When there is very little food for them the plants will be weak and bear little in the way of flower, fruit, or seed, as compared with the far stronger and better-yielding plants that grow on the surrounding moist 'surface soil'.

The soil of any country can quickly grow poor, if it is left neglected for a long time. That unfortunately is what happened in Sind and the Western Punjab long ages ago. Owing probably to wars, the people ran away from the Indus Valley, leaving their fields uncultivated, and their forests were cut down or destroyed in other ways. The top soil was left bare and patches of desert began to appear.

Deserts spread easily. When there is no vegetation to protect it the surface soil loses its moisture by evaporation and quickly turns dry. The strong winds that sweep over it are able to blow away the tiny pieces of dry soil and carry them far away. We are all familiar with duststorms and have often felt the sting of sand in our faces as the wind rushes past us. The hot *loo* blowing from the south and west in the N.W.F.P. and the Western Punjab contains so much sand and dust that sometimes the sun is hidden by what looks like a greyish-yellow curtain. Much of that 'dust' is the precious top soil. Bit by bit the 'good soil' is lost.

It is not only the wind that harms the surface of our soil. Heavy rainfall in places where grass or trees are absent can also carry it away. Although rain is scarce in Western Pakistan, when it does fall it can come in the form of great showers which wash the top soil away. There is nothing there to prevent the water from rushing into the rivers and taking the rich earth with it.

Thus 'erosion' (or rubbing away) by both wind and water has been taking place for hundreds of years over wide areas, changing what were once the fertile tracts of the Indus Valley into desert or semi-desert country. It is a fact noticed all over the world that rain falls more abundantly on cultivated and forest land than on bare land. It seems to avoid deserts. The less the rainfall, the more scanty the vegetation in or near the desert, which is thus able to spread in all directions. The Sahara, the Gobi, the Arabian, and Persian Deserts were once well covered with grass and trees, but during the last two or three thousand years these deserts have become much larger. They are now completely sandy rainless regions through which no great rivers flow.

Man, however, may be able to restore the deserts to fertility. He has first, however, to make a mighty effort to bring back moisture in the soil. He cannot create rain; yet he can stop the desert from spreading by bringing water to it from rivers or from wells, thus keeping the edges of the desert properly covered with green vegetation. Bit by bit —almost yard by yard—he can plant trees and crops farther and farther into the desert. Not only does the soil by that means become protected from the sweeping winds, but the region can again begin to attract rainfall.

We are fortunate in Western Pakistan because we still have great quantities of water available with which to fight and conquer the desert. We have the water which flows in seven great rivers, the Indus and its tributaries (the Kabul, the Jhelum, the Chenab, the Ravi, the Beas, and the Sutlej). These rivers rise in the high mountains, where the snow falls heavily in winter and melts all through the summer. Even when our monsoon rainfall is light, the seven rivers are able to bring enough water to the plains of Pakistan, and there is no fear that they will ever run dry.

Under the soil of Western Pakistan we also have enormous hidden stores of water, which is really rain that has sunk deep into the earth, and which we can obtain by tube wells. Also we still have a small amount of monsoon rainfall. By making proper use of all this water with the help of great canal and irrigation channels, and by spreading the moisture over the land, we should be able to cover the country with its natural protective coat of greenery. In time the millions of acres which are newly coming under cultivation may attract better rainfall. At least, however, we are slowly winning the battle against the deserts in Sind, Bahawalpur, and Thal. We can succeed also in Baluchistan.

There is one more way in which we can protect our

THE SOIL AND ITS PROTECTION

soil and keep it fertile. We already know that plants take their food through their roots. Every season, therefore, land on which crops have been grown loses some part of the organic matter and chemicals contained in the top soil. These have been used up in feeding the plants. If these substances are not replaced, the soil naturally becomes poorer and poorer, until a time comes when there is not enough 'food' left in it to keep our plants strong and healthy. Does not something like that happen also to us? If we keep on taking grain from a basket, a time will come when we must buy some more grain or go hungry, because the basket will be empty.

Unfortunately, for long ages our cultivators were so ignorant that in many parts of the country they did not know how to put back into the soil the 'food' which the crops had used. One of the most valuable of organic substances in the top soil consists of cattle droppings. Instead of drying this natural manure, spreading it over the fields, and digging it back into the soil, our people often used it as fuel for burning. They mixed it with straw and mud to serve as fuel for cooking purposes. They still do this far and wide. The result is that many fields never have their natural richness restored. They keep on losing their 'plant food' year after year, and the cultivators find that the crops become thinner and weaker.

In more recent years, however, our Pakistanis have begun to learn that they must spread manure over the soil. They have seen on demonstration farms what a wonderful difference there is between a properly manured field and an exhausted unmanured field. They have been shown how that same cattle-dung and straw can be dug into the soil and produce crops that are thrice as good—

instead of being wasted as fuel for their cooking stoves.

Since fuel is, of course, necessary in our homes, we should make every effort to grow firewood. There would be no need to burn the valuable cattle-dung if only every village set aside a few acres of land for firewood, which can be grown quickly and cheaply. Our country contains only a small amount of coal, which also costs too much for the villagers. But there is enough land to supply every village with all the firewood it requires. All that has to be done is to keep on explaining to our ryots how much they will gain through better crops. We can all help to educate them.

Through the use of demonstration farms, our peasants are also learning that chemical manures, such as ammonium sulphate, potash, and lime, can help them to grow better crops. Artificial manures, however, cannot altogether replace the organic manures which Nature has provided.

When all our fields are properly watered, manured, and tended, and more and more 'good land' cultivated, Pakistan will be able to grow the finest crops of wheat, rice, cotton, jute, sugar-cane, and oilseeds in the world. We will be able to provide abundance of food for ourselves and for other countries.

CHAPTER XII

OUR CROPS AND OUR LIVESTOCK

ALREADY in both Eastern and Western Pakistan we grow crops worth hundreds of millions of rupees each year. Let us now examine in greater detail the nature and situation of the chief crops, and think also of the great numbers of animals and poultry which we keep and which also help to bring a great deal of wealth into our country.

There are two kinds of crops—known as 'food crops' and 'money crops'. As the names show, the 'food crops' are those that provide things that we can eat—wheat, rice, barley, maize, *jowar, bajra,* pulses (*dal*), tea, fruit, sugar-cane and betel-nut, coco-nuts, and spices; also grain and grass fodder for our livestock. We have many millions of animals and farmyard birds which we have to feed. These creatures are of value to us in many ways.

The 'money crops' are those which we cannot use as food, but which we can make into useful articles or sell to other people. Our cotton, jute, indigo, tobacco, oil-seeds, timber and bamboo, mulberry trees, and many other items mean a vast amount of wealth to our country. Whenever any of these crops fail, our people suffer great hardship and loss. It would be impossible for so large a population as our eighty millions to live without them.

Let us consider also, not only the direct importance of all the foodstuffs and merchandise to us as human beings, but the indirect value of some of them. Grain, grass, and dry fodder for our cattle, our horses, our sheep, our goats, and even the humble donkey, are items which we cannot neglect because of the value of these creatures. When alive our domesticated animals do a great deal of work for us. Our bullocks help to till the fields and carry away the crops. Our horses provide us with cheap transport. Our milch cows and goats yield us milk, butter, and ghee in vast quantities; the donkey, as our builders know, is a very useful beast of burden. Our sheep give us wool for our winter clothing and our blankets. Goats' hair is put to many uses. Nor should we forget that 'ship of the desert', the camel, which plays such an important part in transport throughout Western Pakistan.

Even when no longer alive, all these animals still provide us with wealth in one form or another. Our cattle, sheep, and goats become food for millions. Their hides and skins fetch good prices when tanned and made into shoes, saddles, bags, trunks, purses, and numerous other useful articles. Even their bones are not wasted, becoming converted into valuable manure for our fields. Buffalo horns are made into knife handles or carved ornaments. There is also a large trade in bristles of various kinds for the manufacture of brushes.

Our livestock includes millions of ducks, hens, and geese. These too not only furnish us with eggs, but with eatable flesh. Their feathers are used as stuffing for mattresses and pillows.

Like ourselves, all these creatures depend on food grown on our land. They are well worth all the care we can give them. Our experts are not satisfied merely with good conditions, but are always trying to improve the size and quality of our domesticated animals. For this purpose there are special breeding farms where the best stud animals are kept. Some are imported bulls, stallions (horses), and rams, which are crossbred with local animals. By this means, we have obtained a better milk yield from cows, and also stronger bullocks. Arab, English, and Australian strains have helped to improve our own country-bred horses.

Improvements are also being made in wool production by breeding better sheep in the North-West Frontier Province, Baluchistan, and Sind.

Here are some figures to show how large are the numbers of our domesticated livestock in Pakistan:—

	Millions
Oxen	$24\frac{1}{4}$
Buffaloes	$5\frac{1}{2}$
Sheep	6
Goats	10
Horses	$\frac{1}{2}$
Donkeys and mules	1
Camels	$\frac{1}{2}$
Fowls	24
Ducks	5

While our soil has to support all these creatures, it has also to produce food for 80 million human beings and, if possible, some surplus food to sell to other countries. There is little wonder that agriculture is our chief occupation. Mention has already been made of our principal 'food crops', and we should learn more about these.

Rice ranks first in importance, because it is the chief food of the population of Eastern Pakistan. Almost all is grown there, but there are also some rice-fields in Lower Sind. The total harvest of both areas is on an average about 8 million tons, which is only just enough for the local population. The acreage is about 23 millions.

Wheat forms the chief food of Western Pakistan, and is grown only in that part of our country. The climate of Eastern Pakistan is too warm and too wet for this crop. The total production is about $32\frac{1}{2}$ lakhs of tons, of which 24 lakhs is used by the local population; the surplus of 8 lakhs is exported. The acreage under wheat is 10,750,000.

Gram, largely used for feeding livestock, is grown on 31 million acres in both East and West Pakistan; the annual yield is about 700,000 tons, mostly from Western Pakistan.

Bajra, jowar, maize, and barley are produced chiefly in Western Pakistan, where the variety of crops is greater. Eastern Bengal concentrates on the cultivation of rice.

Sugar-cane production has recently increased. The crop is grown in both Eastern and Western Pakistan. A great new sugar factory (one of the largest in Asia) has now been built at Mardan (N.W.F.P.), and is able to produce annually 50,000 tons of pure crystal sugar. Much of the sugar used by the local population in Eastern Bengal consists of *jaggery*. Pakistan does not yet make enough sugar for its own needs. This crop takes a good deal of 'plant food' out of the soil, and growers therefore have to manure the land more freely to prevent it from becoming exhausted.

Among our many 'cash crops', jute is the most valuable. Nearly all the jute produced in the world is grown in Eastern Pakistan, because here we have the most suitable combination of conditions: a damp soil, moist weather, and periodic floods, which spread rich natural organic manure over the fields.

OUR CROPS AND OUR LIVESTOCK

Four-fifths of the jute-producing areas of the Indo-Pakistan continent are in our province of Eastern Bengal. The best and finest qualities of jute grow only in that region. Our jute districts are Mymensingh, Dacca, Comilla, Faridpur, Pabna, Bogra, and parts of Rangpur. Some jute is grown in Bharat, but it is Pakistan that supplies the world's needs.

The jute plant grows well even in standing water. It often grows to a height of twelve feet. Cut before becoming fully ripe, the plants are retted in water for about three weeks. The fibre is then separated by beating and washing. March to May is sowing time; the jute harvest is ready between July and September.

When the fibre has been removed, it is dried and then pressed into bales weighing 400 lb. each. The bales are taken by boat or train to the jute mills near Calcutta, where it is spun into yarn (or thread). It is next woven into gunny cloth, which is used for making the gunny bags for packing rice, wheat, oilseeds, and other grains. Some of the gunny is made into coarse cloth and rugs. Jute is also made into rope and twine. The fibre is very strong.

Nearly all our jute is exported. The chief buyers are Bharat and the United Kingdom, both of which have a great number of factories. Owing to the way in which the 1947 Partition took place, Pakistan at first did not possess a single jute factory of its own, whereas there were over 100 factories in Bharat. Now, however, Pakistan has built two large factories at Chittagong as well as about 35 baling presses in the districts. Chittagong and the new port of Chalna export $2\frac{1}{2}$ million bales annually to the United Kingdom, the United States of America, Europe, and Japan. Pakistan's jute is worth Rs. 125 crores each year. No wonder we call it 'the Golden Fibre'.

Almost as important is our cotton crop, which is grown in Western Pakistan. Very little is produced in Eastern Pakistan, where the climate is not suitable. The cotton provinces are Sind and West Punjab, famed for their rich dark soils. Here we find the best qualities of this precious crop, 'the Silver Fibre'. Of the total area of about 3 million acres under cotton, 2,600,000 grow the long-stapled American varieties, and less than half a million acres are given over to the short-stapled *desi* cottons. In a good year Pakistan produces 1,200,000 bales (of 400 lb. each) of cotton, valued at Rs. 50 crores. The yield is slightly greater even than that of Egypt, world-famed for its cotton crop. Only in the United States, Soviet Russia, Bharat, China, and Brazil is the annual crop larger. When our new irrigation schemes are completed, it is more than possible that Pakistan will take its place among the first three producers of raw cotton.

Much of our cotton is exported to Bharat, Japan, the United Kingdom, France, Italy, Czechoslovakia, Belgium, and Holland. Very little is manufactured into yarn and cloth in our own factories, because in pre-Partition days nearly all the cotton spinning and weaving factories were situated in the provinces which are now in Bharat. Whereas Bombay, the Central Provinces, and the United Provinces contained hundreds of factories, we did not have a single large cotton mill in Pakistan when the Partition took place. Even within our first three years of existence we have built at least five splendid new factories —two at Karachi, and one each at Multan, Lyallpur, and Rahimyarkhan. Several more will be added quickly, including a large mill in Eastern Bengal and an extremely large one near Karachi.

OUR CROPS AND OUR LIVESTOCK

Knowing how important it is that our country should make its own cloth, instead of exporting the raw cotton to other lands and then receiving it back in the form of piece-goods, our Government has prepared great plans for our cotton growers and manufacturers. Much machinery is being bought, and Pakistan's Central Cotton Committee is helping in many ways to make sure that our country grows the finest qualities of fibre and makes for itself all the cloth that we require. Great care is also being taken to see that there is no mixing of American and *desi* seeds. Steps are also being taken to destroy the various insect pests that harm our cotton crop. Large numbers of expert workers are being trained for every department of our valuable cotton industry.

Karachi is our great cotton port. From here hundreds of big ships carry the bales to Bharat and dozens of other countries. In an ordinary year over 800,000 bales are exported from Karachi.

Tea, although used for brewing a refreshing drink, cannot be looked upon as strictly a 'food crop'. It is exported in large quantities from Pakistan, and is therefore classified as a 'money crop'. As compared with some other countries, especially Great Britain and Australia, Pakistanis do not drink much tea. It will probably become more popular here in course of time.

The tea bush first grew in China, where for centuries it was a closely guarded secret. Nearly a hundred years ago some of the seeds were brought to British India, and were planted in Assam and Sikkim. The lower mountains there receive much monsoon rainfall and the climate is suitable, being neither too hot nor too cold. Sylhet was also found to be a very favourable district for tea cultivation. Sylhet district was given to us at the 1947 Partition, and nearly all Pakistan's tea is produced there. Small amounts are grown also in the Chittagong and Tippera districts.

On the tea gardens the tea bushes grow to a height of only 3 or 4 feet. They are planted about 8 feet apart in long straight rows, with a few small trees to give them some shade. The picking of the leaves is done very carefully. Only a few new leaves are taken from each bush every few days. Gangs of men, women, and children earn their living in this way. They are paid according to the weight of the leaves in their baskets. The picking season lasts from May to December.

The tea plantations are owned chiefly by companies, who have built many factories in which the leaves are dried and prepared for market. They are sorted according to size and quality, and are then packed in wooden chests and sent by boat or train to Chittagong, for export to Europe, Australia, and other parts of the world.

In the year 1949–50, Pakistan sold about 27 million lb. of tea to other countries for nearly 400 lakhs of rupees. It is fortunate that the great Assam earthquake of 1950, which destroyed many tea gardens in Bharat, did very little harm to our plantations and factories in Sylhet.

Timber is not yet one of the sufficiently developed products of Pakistan. Our forests cover only 14,500 square miles (or 6·4 per cent of the total land). They are found chiefly in Eastern Bengal, but cover a very small area in Western Pakistan. Many other countries have given over a far bigger proportion of their land to forests, which bring them great wealth. Finland, Norway, Sweden, European Russia, Newfoundland, and other countries are examples. They look after their forests very carefully, and always plant more trees in place of those that are cut down. We need to train many more foresters. This is a splendid career for those young men who love an open-air life and adventure.

Pakistan makes much use of wood for buildings, bridges, railway sleepers, furniture, paper manufacture, and boat construction. Plans are being made to plant forests in many more places. When they grow they will be a great gain to our country. Forests are valuable, not only for their timber, but because they act as screens against strong winds and thus save our soil. They also seem to attract better rainfall. It should be the ambition of every Pakistani boy and girl to plant at least one tree every year. We would soon have tens of millions of trees.

Among other forest or plantation trees we should not forget bamboos, coco-nut palms, date-palms, and rattan canes. All these can be made into useful goods both for our own use and for export.

We should notice also that our country grows no less than 140,000 tons of tobacco every year—mostly in Eastern Pakistan. This is a valuable 'money crop', and if we grew still more tobacco of good quality our peasants would gain a great deal of extra money through bigger exports.

Other 'cash crops' which are already being grown in good quantities are linseed, rape and mustard seed, and sesame. From these various oils are manufactured. These oils are used as lubricants for machinery and for the making of paints. There is a huge demand for lubricating oil in all parts of the world, and it would pay Pakistan to grow a larger quantity of oilseeds.

CHAPTER XIII

OUR INDUSTRIES

PAKISTAN is not yet a land of great industries. We have a few large factories and many small ones, but we are still a nation of farmers. The care of our fields and livestock has for centuries been almost the sole occupation of our people. Even in the days of British rule, there was very little change in this general system. To-day, out of our 80 million inhabitants, only about 400,000 depend on real workshops for their livelihood. Even if we add our building labourers, our railway hands, boatmen, dockyard workers, and canal diggers, there remain about 75 million men, women, and children whose lives are bound up with the fields.

There are many other countries of the world somewhat like ourselves, especially the 'younger' countries, where the cultivation of crops is still the chief occupation. They grow food and raw materials for the industrial countries, which are sometimes so busy making finished goods that they do not grow enough food for themselves.

Warm countries are the only places were certain crops grow in sufficient quantities. Cotton and jute, for example, can be cultivated only in tropical climates. So also tea, rubber, tobacco, sugar-cane, rice, and most oilseeds. Having large quantities of these to spare, agricultural countries gladly sell them to other countries in exchange for manufactured articles such as machinery, cloth, steel, household goods, motor-cars, radio sets, and other useful products.

OUR INDUSTRIES

All the same, it is the aim of most countries to make things for themselves out of the raw materials which the people produce. They seek to avoid needless expense caused by having to import articles made out of what their own fields, forests, and mines have produced. We have seen, for example, that Pakistan grows a great deal of raw cotton, but that nearly all our cotton cloth has to be sent to us from other countries. This is because we had practically no cotton factories of our own when our country was created in 1947. In the same way we had no great engineering works (except for our railway wagon and repair works), no jute mills, no big tanneries, no tobacco factories, no chemical factories, no shipbuilding yards, and no plastic factories. We could not make our own bicycles, motor-cars, rubber tyres, aeroplanes, or radio sets. All the big cotton and jute mills were on the Bharat side of the 1947 boundary line; so were the sugar factories, the tanneries, the iron and steel foundries, and the great engineering works.

Pakistan was further handicapped by having no really big coalfields, while only a comparatively small quantity of petroleum was being produced by our oil-wells.

It soon became understood that our people could not grow really prosperous and raise their general standard of living by depending on crops alone. Why should we continue to pay the cost of buying manufactured goods from abroad, if we could make some portion of these in our own land, especially if they were made out of raw materials which came from our own fields? For example, there were all those millions of bales of cotton and jute going to Bharat and other countries and coming back to us in the form of yarn or cloth or gunny. We had plenty of men willing and able to work. All that was needed was to give them the tools, teach them how to use the tools, make our own machinery, and start making everything possible ourselves.

Our Government decided that Pakistan could not prosper on agriculture alone, but must develop her manufactures. The first step was to let it be known that anyone willing to start factories or workshops would be free to do so and would receive our Government's help in all possible ways. Industrial works need big sums of money for the building of the necessary workshops and offices, for the purchase of machinery, the payment of salaries to experts, and purchase of raw materials. People who had the capital were encouraged to invest it for industrial purposes, and foreign capital was welcomed. The Government set up the State Bank of Pakistan, and lent big sums of money to people who were able to build factories and create work. Laws were made to help great companies to search for more coal and petroleum.

During the first three years of Pakistan's existence, hundreds of clever young Pakistanis were sent to English and American universities and factories for special training. They are now returning full of knowledge about how to arrange and manage our various industries. Our own technical and engineering schools were improved and enlarged. Where necessary, experts and teachers were brought from Europe and America to show our own men how to go about their work.

Side by side with all this, our Government set up many committees to examine each industry in detail, and to draw up careful plans for every step that had to be taken. Research stations and laboratories were built, to test materials and to improve our methods. A search was also begun for new minerals, and some important discoveries were made. We now know much more than formerly about the various materials that we have, how to make all kinds of goods, how to sell them in the best markets, and how to train our industrial workers.

A big problem soon arose: how to provide enough power to work all the machinery with which our factories will be equipped. Pakistan has no big coal-mines, and some of our coal is not of good quality. Our petroleum fields also are not yet yielding enough fuel. Our electric-power stations at present depend mostly on fuel, and do not produce enough electricity for all our coming needs.

One of the first things, therefore, was to plan the construction of hydro-electric stations. At these the strength and speed of falling water (in our rivers and canals) will be used for setting huge turbines in motion, by which much more electric power will be generated. In addition, some of the power stations will use Diesel oil; others will use steam from coal-burners. In our first three years our supply of electricity has been more than doubled. Much greater increases will soon follow.

We should make a special note of two very great electric projects which are being planned. One of these will be the Warsak Dam, which is to be built across the Kabul River, in the N.W.F.P. It is expected to provide enough electric power not only for all the factories that will rise in that province, but also for the electrification of our railways, buses, and trolleys. The other is the Karnafuli Project in Eastern Pakistan, which will provide electric power in Chittagong. Both these schemes will also help to improve irrigation, because great new canals will start from there.

The search for big sources of petroleum is still going on in both East and West Pakistan. At present the total production of crude oil is nearly one million barrels a year. Better coal deposits may also be found. For some years to come, however, Pakistan's industries will have to depend chiefly on electric power.

Iron is the metal of which Pakistan makes the greatest use. Much of it has to be imported. We have some small iron-mines, situated in the N.W.F.P. and Baluchistan, but the ore is not of very good quality. Nearly all our steel, which is obtained from iron containing a very small quantity of carbon, comes to us from other countries. About 11,000 tons of steel is manufactured each year in Lahore and Karachi. Pakistan now uses more than 260,000 tons of iron and steel a year, of which only 60,000 tons are produced in our own country.

Yet the art of casting metals is not entirely new to our people. They knew how to do it at Tatta (seventy miles east of Karachi) hundreds of years ago, and made good swords and other weapons. In our own day, however, iron and steel are put to many other uses. These metals are required for our railway lines, locomotives, wagons, and carriages, for our buildings and bridges, our motor-vehicles, our oil engines, our heavy pipes, our wire fencing, ploughs and other agricultural implements, water tanks, storage bins, for our machinery and electric motors, as well as for a great many military purposes. Our armoured cars, artillery, shells, rifles, and bayonets need large quantities of steel. In the form of thin sheets, steel is made into 'tins' as containers for oil. The bicycles on which we ride to school are made of steel. One of our first cares, therefore, is to set up more steel and iron works in Pakistan so that we can make as much as possible ourselves—from the smallest steel screw to the biggest steel boiler.

It will be many years before Pakistan is able to manufacture all its own steel requirements. Meanwhile, we cannot wait, and therefore we have to buy machinery and tools from other lands. We have to set up so many different industries as quickly as possible. More textile mills, for example, are urgently wanted—especially cotton and jute factories.

As we have already seen, Pakistan did not possess a single jute mill when the 1947 Partition took place. We could make none of our own jute into gunny or cordage. At first we did not have even enough presses for making *pukka* bales. Our Government quickly bought more presses, which are already working. A few small mills for weaving jute into hessian cloth and for making gunny bags have recently been built in Eastern Pakistan, and some very large ones are being planned for Narayanganj and Chittagong.

Jute is used, not only for ordinary gunny and twine, but for tarpaulins (large waterproof coverings), tents, carpets, rugs, linoleum floor coverings, chair covers, and finer qualites of twine and cord. Even although for the present we make only the coarser jute goods, there is room for dozens of factories in Eastern Bengal.

In 1947 the Partition left us with only fourteen cotton mills in Pakistan (nine in East Bengal, four in West Punjab and one in Sind). As a contrast, hundreds of cotton mills went to Bharat's share—in Bombay, Sholapur, Ahmedabad, Surat, Nagpur, Cawnpore, Delhi, Amritsar, Calcutta, and many other places. Our eighty million people in Pakistan have to buy enormous quantities of cloth from Bharat, the U.K., America, Japan, and various European countries, only because our own mills are too few and too small to supply even a tiny fraction of our needs. Half our total imports, in fact, consist of cotton goods. The same ships which sail from Karachi laden with our raw cotton return to us with huge cargoes of that same cotton made up in the form of cloth.

It is only natural that we should wish to make our own cotton into piece-goods by our own efforts. Our Government is doing its best to bring this about, and has arranged a plan which will bring good progress in the next few years. None of our provinces will then be without a large cotton factory. Already one-fourth of our entire industrial population is engaged in cotton ginning factories, baling presses, and mills. A few years hence, it is expected, nearly a quarter of a million Pakistanis will be earning their living from the manufacture of cotton goods.

There are great hopes also of improving the woollen industry, which has been carried on successfully for many years in Pakistan. Our best wool-bearing sheep are in Sind, Baluchistan, and the N.W.F.P., and they yield about twenty-eight million pounds of raw wool each year. Of this quantity Pakistan exports about twenty million pounds to other countries, chiefly the United States and Great Britain. The remaining six million pounds is woven by our own people into blankets, coarse tweeds, carpets, rugs, *namdahs,* and blanketing cloth. The better qualities of woollen cloth, suitable for clothing (knitted or woven), still have to be imported.

Owing to the 1947 Partition our country had no woollen mills to start with, as all the existing factories were on the Bharat side. Most of our own production was, and still is, carried on as 'cottage industries'. Our

Government, however, has now built two fairly large woollen mills at its own cost, and some privately owned mills have also begun work. Warm clothing is a necessity in most parts of Western Pakistan, because the winters there are very cold. In Eastern Pakistan, however, the people need to use light shawls and blankets for only a few weeks between November and February, because they have a much milder climate.

Other important industries are the manufacture of paper, leather goods, rubber goods, electrical goods, chemicals, glassware, cement, pottery, porcelain, light machinery, soap, and sports goods. These are already being carried on in large or small factories scattered all over Pakistan. All these lines can be developed and made to provide work for many more people. Our chemical factories manufacture fertilizers for our fields and thus play a big part in the welfare of our country.

In addition, a large number of industries of many different kinds are carried on in the homes of our people or in very small workplaces which are not large enough to be called factories. Such industries are known as 'cottage industries'. Among the best known are silk-weaving, hand-spinning and weaving (Dacca muslins may yet regain their ancient fame), the making of sports goods, hospital equipment, musical instruments, glass bangles, household utensils, *niwar,* brushware, carpets and rugs, glue, ivory carving, lacquer work, pottery, mat-making, cane work, horn or shell work, tanning, *gur*-making, woodwork, brassware, and enamelling.

Although as a rule only the members of a family are thus occupied, sometimes a few apprentices and skilled persons are also employed in this class of industry. Each home may turn out only a small quantity of goods, but taken together the output is of very great value. Cottage industries are carried on in this way in all our provinces, and provide a living for lakhs of workers. With better training in the use of simple machinery, they could produce more and better goods, and thus help our country on the road to prosperity; the Government are providing more technical schools and helping our cottage workers in many other ways.

All these facts enable us to realize that Pakistan is making promising progress. It may never become as highly industrialized a land as England, where there are many thousands of great factories and millions of skilled workers, with crowded towns and cities, where the sky is darkened with smoke. Perhaps we do not want that, and are happy to see our huge fields properly cultivated. Yet we wish also to make far more of the goods that we use in our daily lives. Each of us can help our factories and cottage industries by 'buying Pakistani products' and thus increasing the earnings of our workers even while we avoid the cost of needless imports.

CHAPTER XIV

CO-OPERATIVE SOCIETIES

ONE of the most successful ways by which our ryots and cottage workers can become more prosperous is co-operation. What one man cannot do by himself can be done by several working together. That is just what co-operation means: 'working together' or 'joint effort'.

We see this everywhere in our daily lives. Our homes are the simplest examples. The family is the smallest co-operative unit. Father and sons go out to work in the fields or factories and earn the money with which our rent is paid and our food and clothing purchased. They also help with various jobs that have to be done in or about the house—the mending of roofs or doors, the carrying of heavy articles, the chopping up of wood. Mother and daughters attend to the preparation of food, the cleansing of household utensils, the making and mending of clothes, and often light work in the fields. By the joint efforts of all, each doing his or her own share and helping the others, the family carries out all the things that need to be done for a happy and comfortable home. That is one form of 'co-operation'.

Outside the family, we see much the same idea used in the affairs of our village or town. There are so many things which even the strongest man cannot manage to do alone. If he has to build his house, he often requires the help of three or four other people. His neighbours and friends willingly give him a helping hand; they know that when necessary he will also come along to help them in digging a well or cutting down a tree or ploughing a field. Or in a town they may help him to put together some machinery, knowing that he in his turn will help them in carrying their goods to market.

So far our examples have been concerned only with joint efforts in everyday life. The same simple idea is easily adopted in other ways which mean something more than merely bodily labour. Co-operation is just as useful in managing our business affairs together for our common good. It means the grouping of a number of persons, each with only a small amount of money, but with the same aim in view, into a society which works together to obtain that object for all equally.

An example or two will help us to see how this is done. Let us suppose that in a certain district there are fifty families which have to buy various household goods from nearby towns. They find that it costs much money to travel there often and that they have sometimes to pay rather high prices for the goods. They know that if they could buy a big quantity of such articles in one lot they would obtain wholesale prices which would save them money. In the first place they could perhaps buy a bale of cloth and share it out amongst themselves, and in that way have to pay less for each yard.

A number of them like this idea and meet to discuss it. They tell others about it, and at last it is decided that, if each of the fifty families lends a few rupees towards the cost, several rolls of cloth of different qualities and patterns could be bought direct from a factory or merchant at a cheaper rate than from a retail shop. Then each family could buy as many yards as it needs from the common stock at a price lower than a trader's. As this method saves money, most of the families agree to the idea and offer to advance a few rupees each towards the capital needed. A committee of four or five people is formed, and this committee attends to the buying and selling of the cloth in such a way as to make a small profit for all and at the same time to sell the cloth more cheaply than the shops.

In other words, a 'Co-operative Consumers' Society' has been formed in that village. It has 'shares' of a few rupees each. Each member of the society can buy one or more shares. The society can buy and sell not only cloth, but many other articles which the villagers or townsfolk use daily. Our Co-operative Consumers' Societies are able to open their own shops, where prices are a little lower than in the markets. They supply such things as oil, sugar, grain, and other foodstuffs; tinned goods; paints; tools for farmers or carpenters; seeds; toys; leather goods; knives; books and paper; ready-made clothing; bicycles, and electrical goods. At Lahore, Karachi, and some other big towns, the Central Co-operative Stores carry on a great deal of business, and import useful manufactured goods at lower prices from Britain, America, and other western countries, as well as from makers in Pakistan itself.

Co-operative Societies can take other forms. Among the most useful are our Co-operative Marketing Societies, which help our peasants and cottage workers to sell their produce at the best prices and with the least possible trouble and expense. Agricultural smallholders gain many benefits if they are members of such a society. For example, in one district there may be several farmers who keep poultry and wish to sell the eggs. If each person takes his few dozen eggs to the market town he has to make the journey there and back, or perhaps sell them at too low a price to a local shopkeeper. The farmer's gain is very small, and he does not feel encouraged to keep more hens. But if there is a Co-operative Marketing Society it can buy all the eggs from all the local farmers and sell them at a reasonable price to the big shops and consumers' societies in the towns and cities, or direct to hotels and shipping companies. This saves the farmers much trouble, and gives them a better income from their poultry-keeping. They are encouraged to rear more hens and earn better money.

In the same way other producers can easily group themselves into Co-operative Marketing Societies. Cottage workers who make small articles such as embroidery, gold and silver thread, toys, knitted goods, home-woven cloth, sports goods, leather goods (shoes, purses, wallets, harness, boxes, and straps), wood carvings, enamel ware, and pottery can join such societies and sell all their products readily to them and thereby obtain better prices than in the open market. The Co-operative Marketing Societies make their profit by selling these articles where they are needed. All the members share the profit.

Co-operative Banks have also been formed all over Pakistan. There is a large one in the N.W.F.P., with branches in all the districts. There are 28 Co-operative Banks and Banking Unions in the Western Punjab; 83 in Eastern Bengal, with 10 Land Mortgage Banks; and some also in Sind. These societies give the local farmers, civil servants, traders, and manufacturers a way to save money and to put it to good use. They lend capital for new industries, and by this means help our country to become more prosperous.

In addition, we have a very large number of Agricultural Societies. They have in the past lent many crores of rupees to farmers, to enable them to buy their own land, farming implements, seeds, and livestock, or to construct wells. They have also helped to provide capital for such useful works as ginning factories and baling presses. As they charge very low interest, they have saved many farmers from falling into the clutches of money-lenders. They have also helped large numbers to pay off debts which would otherwise have ruined them.

We all know what a curse the *baniya* (banker) was to our peasants in pre-Partition days. He used to take advantage of the poverty and ignorance of all classes of people and charge them such high rates of interest for loans that they were never able to pay back the money. Often the borrower could not even pay the interest, which kept on adding to the amount owed. Nearly every rupee of the borrower's pay or earnings went to the money-lender, and often there was no escape. His crops were heavily mortgaged even before he had sowed his seed or reaped his harvest. There was little left for a poor farmer to live on. In olden days even his property itself was seized.

Agricultural Co-operative Societies are now to be found all over Pakistan. There are 10,000 of them in the Western Punjab, with 800,000 members; about 1,000 of them in the N.W.F.P., with over 100,000 members; nearly 30,000 societies in Eastern Bengal, and some also in Sind. They have been very helpful in giving our Muslim refugees from Bharat a chance to become successful farmers, because they have been able to provide them with loans.

Mention should also be made of those Co-operative Societies which have carried out the work known as the 'consolidation of holdings', especially in the Western Punjab. It should be explained that, owing to the olden laws of property, when a land-holder died his land was divided equally among his children, and when these died each of their small-holdings was split up in the same way. With this subdivision going on for generations, the pieces of land left to many holders in recent times became so small and so badly scattered that they could not be properly cultivated. The consolidation societies arranged exchanges of the plots of land, so that each person was able to have his holding all in one large piece. In the Western Punjab alone half a million acres have been rearranged in this way and the peasants have been saved much trouble. Our ryots in Eastern Bengal and Sind need to make much more use of such a good system.

Our towns and cities suddenly became very crowded just after the 1947 Partition. Tens of thousands of refugees from the Bharat side poured especially into Lahore and Karachi. No houses were left over, and very many people had to live in camps or in the open air. The middle and lower classes in the cities quickly joined together to form Co-operative Housing Societies. By putting their money into these, the 'new-comers' have been able to build nearly 10,000 houses and many more will soon be ready. Singly the people would not have been able to do much building work, but by co-operating with each other they are succeeding. 'Each for all, and all for each', is the motto of the Co-operative Movement.

Our Government fully knows how valuable are the various kinds of Co-operative Societies. Laws have been made for their proper management, and a special Government Department has been set up in each province of our country to help and guide these societies in every possible way. The Government also grants big loans to them through the Co-operative Banks, so that they are able to do their good work with enough capital.

The Co-operative Movement was introduced into what is now Pakistan nearly fifty years ago. Under British rule it spread rapidly at first, but progress later became slow. This was because the *baniya* still had a tight grip on our poorer classes. The *baniya* was willing to lend money for any purpose, and cared only about the highest rate of interest he could squeeze out of the ryot or labourer. The borrower's real welfare did not matter to the *baniya*. Poor people were tempted to spend large sums on weddings and feasts without knowing how to pay either interest or principal. The loans were wasted on extravagant things which they could not properly afford and which brought them no return. The Co-operative Societies, on the other hand, would not willingly lend for wasteful purposes. The *baniya* therefore flourished.

When the 1947 Partition took place, however, the *baniyas* fled to Bharat. Any person who then wanted to borrow money for extravagant spending found that the Co-operative Societies were by no means eager to encourage such waste. They were willing to lend—but the borrower had to show that his credit was good. He could readily obtain a loan from the Co-operative Society, provided he wished to spend the money wisely and in a productive manner. Through this many persons saw how foolish they had been in the past to throw away their money uselessly. They now realized that the Co-operative Society was something better and finer than the greedy *baniya*. If a borrower was granted a co-operative loan, the rate of interest was very small, and repayment was made easier by being spread over a longer period.

Our Co-operative Credit Societies have thus been of

great benefit to our country. They have checked waste and extravagance by removing the temptations which the cunning *baniya* offered. They have opened the eyes of our poorer classes to the wisdom of thrifty living. They have shown the peasant, the labourer, and the small shopkeeper that it is far better to save money than to spend it recklessly on useless *tamasha*. The borrower must prove that his credit is based upon careful living and sound business ideas.

In spite of being stricter than the *baniya* in the granting of loans, our Co-operative Societies have shown themselves merciful and helpful. They have been a good moral influence on our people. It is not surprising, therefore, that since the 1947 Partition they have played a very important part in the life of our nation. They have increased greatly in numbers and in membership. To-day they are helping our people far more than in the days of British rule. Through the Co-operative Movement some very large agricultural and industrial schemes are now being carried out all over Pakistan. There is room for much more progress and development of the co-operative system in all parts of our country.

One real secret of the success of our Co-operative Societies is that they do away with a great number of unnecessary 'middlemen' between the buyer and the seller, between the maker of goods and the user. These societies give back in the form of dividends and interest to the members the profit which formerly went into the pockets of the *baniyas* or dealers. The members feel themselves to be genuine partners and shareholders in all the business of a Co-operative Society. They elect its office-holders and committees, and are able to speak and vote at its general meetings.

CO-OPERATIVE SOCIETIES

Co-operative Societies do not prevent people from starting their own companies or business. There is room for both co-operation and private enterprise side by side. Both are found flourishing together in town or countryside, in Pakistan as well as in other lands. The real difference is that a Co-operative Society gives the poorest person a chance of becoming a member and shareholder. His shares are not bought and sold like 'shares' in a company, and their value therefore remains steady.

The Co-operative Movement has spread enormously in many countries, especially in Europe and America. It has an astonishing amount of support in England, where millions of people are members. Every town and many of the larger villages there have 'Co-operative Stores', where goods of all kinds can be bought. Some of these 'Stores' are huge shops, full of beautiful as well as useful articles for household or garden use—all at moderate prices.

The members are given receipts for all the money they spend in the 'Stores', and every half-year they receive a cash 'dividend', which is really their share of the profits according to the amount of their individual purchases. With these dividends they can buy more shares, on which also they receive interest. In this way their 'capital' keeps on increasing and forms an important part of their savings. There are many members whose share capital grows to £300 or £500 in a few years.

With the help of the money thus saved, the Co-operative Societies in England are able to make cheaply a very large portion of the goods they sell. They have formed a Co-operative Wholesale Society which has built enormous factories where millions of pairs of boots and shoes, millions of articles of clothing, and millions of many other things are manufactured. They produce huge quantities of tinned foods. The 'Stores' contain handsome furniture, radio sets, household utensils, carpets, electrical goods, patent medicines, cigarettes, meat, vegetables, milk, bread, fresh fruit, gardening tools, and many other necessities of daily life. The English Co-operative Movement owns thousands of such shops and gives work to hundreds of thousands of people. It has its own dairy and poultry farms, fruit farms, restaurants, and housing estates. It even has its own coal-mines which supply coal to its factories and to a million homes. All this has been done through the poorest people joining as members and buying their requirements from the Co-operative Stores. The principle of 'Each for all, and all for each', has brought about a great improvement in their condition—as it can also do in Pakistan.

CHAPTER XV

TRANSPORT AND COMMUNICATIONS

ONE of the ways in which man proves himself to be superior to any other living creature is his ability to invent methods of carrying himself and his belongings quicker and farther than his mere body would allow. His arms, although strong, cannot compare with the power of an elephant's trunk or the jaws of a tiger, which can lift up and carry heavy objects. His legs, although muscular, move less swiftly than a deer's, and he cannot run far. Having no wings, he cannot fly.

Man, however, has a well-developed brain, and by using his intelligence and reason he has been able to place himself well above animals and birds. He has found out how to travel farther and quicker than any of them. By pressing a button or pulling a lever or turning a small wheel, he can speed through the air at 600 miles an hour, or cover 5,000 miles without stopping, or sail across wide oceans. His voice, although so weak, can be made to sound 10,000 miles away.

Being civilized people who have studied science and engineering, we understand how these 'miracles' are performed. Yet only 3,000 years ago men were so simple and unthinking that if they had then seen our trains, motor-cars, and aeroplanes, or heard our radio receivers and telephones, they would have fled in terror. It was only when man invented the wheel and learned how to use a lever that he came out of his primitive ways of living and began to take his first step towards civilization.

Pakistan began its life as an independent country with a full knowledge of the scientific wonders of our present age. As we shall see, we were faced with many strange difficulties in 1947; but at any rate our people were familiar with the means of fast travel and bulk carriage of goods. Most of our people had already travelled by railway or motor-bus. Our sailors had been for many voyages on ocean liners and cargo ships. They had learned to think nothing about a train journey from Karachi to Peshawar or from Khulna to Parbatipur. The railways came to our land nearly 100 years ago. Similarly, it had long ceased to be a 'miracle' to receive a letter or a telegram from somebody a thousand miles away.

To-day we take it for granted that we can travel quickly almost anywhere we wish. We should all the same try to think how important it is to our country that it should have a good and complete system of transport and communications.

We have already spoken about the great quantities of goods which Pakistan produces—its cotton, jute, grains, salt, and tea. What would be the use of all these (and many other things) if we could not carry them away from our fields, mines, and workplaces? And how would we be able to obtain our coal, machinery, cloth, and other necessaries of life if they were left to pile up on the jetties at Karachi and Chittagong? All these goods, all our merchandise, have to be kept moving according to plan—and to be distributed over a large country. Some of the items must be moved very quickly to prevent them from going bad: fresh food, for example. The cost of moving

TRANSPORT AND COMMUNICATIONS 115

all these things must not be too high, either; or people would not be able to buy and sell easily. In time of war or flood or some such disaster, the carriage of news, of men, and of goods must be done smoothly and at great speed.

One of the first requirements of a modern country, therefore, is that it should have an efficient system of transport and communications. The country cannot be safe, nor can trade flourish, without quick movement. As we read in the first paragraph of this chapter, man is really a slow and rather weak creature. His brain, however, has taught him how to make use of everything round him and convert these resources into speed and strength. To-day he has conquered time and space by means of machinery and electricity. Marching on foot and carrying goods by bullock-cart would be much too clumsy and slow for our armies now—much too slow also for our business people.

Fortunately, in 1947 Pakistan, both East and West, already possessed railways, roads, and waterways. These are the 'life-lines of progress'. There were already a few aerodromes for our aircraft. Since railways carry easily the biggest number of passengers and goods, they naturally take first place in importance.

Our railways consist of two independent systems. Western Pakistan is served by the North-Western Railway, with a total route length of 5,362 miles (mostly broad-gauge). Eastern Pakistan is served by the Eastern Bengal Railway (1,631 miles, of which two-thirds is broad-gauge and one-third metre-gauge). Both systems belong to the Central Government, which is responsible for their entire upkeep, management, and improvement. There is no direct link between the two railways, for they are a thousand miles apart, with the whole of Bharat lying between. A passenger wanting to travel by train from Western Pakistan to Eastern Pakistan has to cross Bharat, and cannot go all the way in the same train; at the frontier beyond Lahore he has to change into a Bharati train, and again into an Eastern Bengal train when he reaches Calcutta on the Eastern Pakistan frontier.

The North-Western Railway has several main lines and branch lines in the Western Punjab and North-West Frontier Province. The main routes there are between Lahore and Peshawar, Lahore and Multan, Lahore and Bahawalpur, and Peshawar and Multan. Many market towns lying between these central points are linked up by branch lines, which cover that region like a spider's web. From Bahawalpur to Sukkur there is only one main line, which splits into two parallel routes southwards from Sukkur. One important branch railway goes from Sukkur to Quetta. There another branch line goes 440 miles farther west to Zahidan, which is 57 miles inside Iranian territory. These two long branches, however, are narrow-gauge. So also is the famous Khyber Railway, which is a branch line (24 miles long) from Jamrud (beyond Peshawar) to Landikhana on the Pakistan-Afghan border.

The Khyber Railway and other lines running from Rawalpindi to our fortress near the Afghan frontier, as also two short branches of the Quetta Railway, were built by the British to help in guarding the country against invasion. They had been at war against Afghanistan, and these 'strategic railways' were of great value in sending troops and munitions to the Frontier. Although the 'strategic lines' are not profitable in the same way as commercial railways, they are necessary for the protection of Pakistan.

Considering the density of population and the great size and value of the crops, Eastern Pakistan's railway system was not sufficiently developed in the days of British rule. There are three great trunk routes there—from Calcutta to Parbatipur (and beyond, into Bharat); from Dacca northwards via Mymensingh to Bahadurabad; from Chittagong to Sylhet. There are several long links between these. The growth of railways in that province has been hindered by the presence of many wide rivers, which frequently change their course, and by the differences in gauge. So mighty is the size of the Brahmaputra that not a single bridge has been built across it. The Megna River, formed by the joining together of the Ganges and the Brahmaputra, is four times the width of the Indus. Owing to these rivers and the absence of bridges, train ferries are used at several points. Train ferries—large barges fitted with railway tracks on to which the railway wagons are pushed—are towed across to the opposite bank of the river and the wagons are pushed out on to the ghat tracks there. The ferries are big enough to carry thirty wagons at a time.

Plans are being made by our Government to add to our railways in both east and west. First, however, it has been necessary to carry out a great amount of repair work and to manufacture new rolling stock and locomotives. Pakistan's railways were very heavily used during the 1939–45 World War, especially the Eastern Bengal Railway, which carried troops and supplies in vast quantities for the Burma campaign. The lines and wagons suffered much damage, which is taking long to repair, because our railway workshops are not large enough. We can look forward to the day when our railways will expand and be restored to thoroughly good condition. Even to-day, they are carrying greatly increased traffic, and it is a matter for pride that they have a splendid reputation for safety. In the year 1949–50 there was no accident to bring loss of life to any person travelling in a passenger train on Pakistan's railways, although, that year, 121 million passengers used our trains. For this and for the punctual running of trains our railwaymen deserve much praise.

Next in importance are our roads. These also fell into bad condition because they were so heavily used during the 1939–45 World War and the emigrations of 1947–8. The Central and Provincial Governments have been put to a great deal of expense and trouble to repair them. There are in Western Pakistan about 5,000 miles of first-class roads, but only 600 miles in Eastern Pakistan. These have superior surfaces suitable for heavy cart or lorry traffic. In addition, we have about 1,350 miles of second-class metalled roads in Western Pakistan and 1,030 in Eastern Pakistan.

Most of our roads, however, are *kachcha* (30,000 miles in Western and 20,000 miles in Eastern Pakistan). They are used by a total of nearly 32,000 motor-vehicles (cars, buses, lorries, and vans). Although these have rubber tyres, they cause some damage. Far more destructive are the narrow iron tyres of the lakhs of bullock-carts which use the roads. If only these carts could all be fitted with rubber-tyred wheels, it would be far easier to keep our roads in a good state of repair, and more money would be left over for making new roads or for changing *kachcha* roads into metalled ones.

Our villages greatly need better roads, but it is almost

useless to build these until rubber tyres are adopted everywhere by carters. In more advanced countries like the United States, Denmark, Holland, Belgium, France, Great Britain, and Germany, iron tyres were given up many years ago, and all carrying is done by motor-vehicles. The result is that the roads even in the villages stay much longer in good condition. Road tests have shown that one bullock can draw a rubber-tyred cart much farther than a pair of bullocks yoked to an iron-tyred cart, and with far less harm to the road surface. Rubber is soft, whereas iron cuts deep ruts in the best of roads, especially when rain has converted the road-surface into mud.

Pakistan has thousands of miles of rivers which boats, barges, and small steamers can use. There are already good numbers of these, especially in Eastern Bengal. Water transport plays a great part there in helping the ryot to send his produce to the market towns and to the seaports for export. The Eastern Bengal Railway are now placing a small fleet of tugs and barges on the rivers there, and these vessels are already carrying great quantities of jute to Chittagong.

Roads, railways, and rivers all lead eventually to and from our great seaports. In a later chapter we shall read about how the seaports have grown into big cities. Karachi is now as great as Bombay or Calcutta, and is in fact one of the most important centres of trade and communications in Asia. This it owes not only to its position on the main sea-routes between Europe and Asia, but also partly to its value as an airport.

Travel by air has become an ordinary part of modern civilized life. Aeroplanes carry many millions of passengers every year all over the world. They have also become a means of attack or defence in warfare. Even before the World War of 1939-45, Karachi had felt the effects of the growth of civil aviation. A large aerodrome had been constructed there, and aircraft coming from Europe always landed there after flying over Syria, Iraq, and Iran. Its value to the Allied Forces became very great during the 1939-45 War. When the war ended, Karachi Airport remained one of the largest and most important in the world. There were civil aerodromes also at Lahore, Quetta, Hyderabad (Sind), and Multan in Western Pakistan, and at Chittagong, Dacca, and Sylhet in Eastern Pakistan.

Aviation proved its value once again during the mass migration of 1947-8. Many thousands of Muslim officials who had opted for Pakistan, but who were stranded in Delhi and other cities of Bharat, were rescued and brought to Pakistan safely and speedily by aeroplane. During August and September 1948 there were record floods in Upper Sind, and all roads and railways lines between Sind and Baluchistan were cut. A Pakistan air line came to the rescue, and carried passengers and mail, hospital patients and perishable food-stuffs, between Karachi and Quetta until the roads and railways were reopened.

Another interesting event was the starting in 1948 of a special service to carry Haj pilgrims between Karachi and Jedda.

The Government has taken many measures to make a thorough success of air communications. A Civil Aviation Department has been formed. Many improvements have been made at Karachi Airport, where there are also repair shops for aircraft and a training school for aviation officers, engineers, radio-operators, and other experts.

The world's first jet airliner will use Karachi. It is wonderful to think that only a hundred years ago the journey between London and Karachi used to take between three months and two years, whereas to-day our Pakistani aeroplanes weekly cover the distance in twenty-four hours. Although more than 1,000 miles apart, Western and Eastern Pakistan are now brought within a five-hours' flight of each other—jet planes will reduce the journey to three and a half hours. Our businessmen and officials are thus able to go from one end of our country to the other in emergency with no loss of time.

Even when there is no need to go on that long journey, they are able to talk to each other and discuss important affairs by telephone. It is true that the trunk line crosses Bharat, but in these days of radio communications we are independent of the land route. There are powerful radio stations in both Eastern and Western Pakistan, and conversations or radiograms are arranged at any hour of the day or night without interruption or delay. Our high-power transmission stations are at Karachi and Dacca. From Karachi we can talk to London by radio, and we will soon be able to talk to people in New York, 9,000 miles away.

Inside Pakistan itself we have a complete postal and telegraphic system. There is no address in either west or east to which a letter cannot be taken by post or a telegram sent. We have post and telegraph offices in hundreds of our towns and large villages. The total length of our telegraph and telephone wires is now nearly 200,000 miles, forming a network all over the country. We are able to write our telegrams in Urdu or Bengali as well as in English. There are telephone exchanges in Karachi, Lahore, Gujrat, Khanewal, Tandlianwala,

Jhang, Mardan, Lyallpur, Sargodha, Rawalpindi, Peshawar, Multan, Rohri, Quetta, and other towns of Western Pakistan; and at Dacca, Chittagong, Narayanganj, Jessore, Saidpur, Ranghpur, Kushtia, and other Eastern Bengal centres. At present about 15,000 telephones are in use, and that number will soon be doubled.

Besides all this, our country has become a member of the Universal Postal Union, and can send letters, parcels, insured and V.P. articles, and money orders by sea or air mail to any part of the world.

CHAPTER XVI

CITIES, PORTS, AND TOWNS

ALTHOUGH about eighty out of every hundred of our population live in villages or small towns, we as a trading country are naturally interested in the growth and prosperity of our cities and our large towns. They are still few in number, but they have suddenly become more important through the special place they hold in the business life of our country.

Man is a sociable creature. He likes to be near his fellow-men. He has the gifts of speech and hearing so that it is always a pleasure to him to be in close communication with those who can share his work, his fun, and his ways of thinking. Even in very ancient times there were towns and cities whose ruins we find all over the world to-day.

Human beings have to depend upon each other in many ways. Co-operation becomes easier when their homes are close together. In times of war, the large towns can be more easily defended than homesteads or villages scattered over a large area. The place chosen by a king as his capital would of course attract numerous courtiers and their followers, officials, and tradesmen. When big enterprises have to be undertaken, it is preferable to have the workers living together near by. So also it is much more convenient for producers and traders to assemble at a suitably central place in order to sell their goods. There thus grew up fortresses, industrial centres, and market towns. Every civilized country has developed in this way, and Pakistan is no exception.

If we inspect many of our present towns, we shall understand how true this is. Let us take Lahore as an example. Situated on the banks of the Ravi, in the heart of an agricultural district, it owes its rise largely to its geographical position. It stands between the Frontier passes and the cities of the Ganges Plain. The river has fords, and the best place for armies to cross was at Lahore. What could be more natural, therefore, than that even in olden days the rulers should build forts at that point so as to stop any invader from passing?

Later at Lahore the Emperor Shah Jehan built a great fort, whose walls are still standing. The city itself was surrounded with walls, which have not yet completely disappeared. To supply the troops it was necessary to have camp followers and many workmen to make weapons and munitions. Hence Lahore also became gradually an industrial centre, to which artisans and craftsmen thronged. By road or river, the surrounding agriculturists would bring their grain and meat. Here also were customers for the merchants, anxious to sell their cloth and ornaments. Lahore thus developed into a great market centre.

Much the same has been the history of our other large towns—Karachi, Dacca, Chittagong, Peshawar, and Quetta. Military needs, work, and trade have caused their rise. Besides these, we have several other towns, which are steadily increasing in size and growing in importance. The six specially named owe their prosperity chiefly to their particularly good geographical positions. Several others, too, may soon develop and some day become nearly as prominent. Sialkot, Hyderabad (Sind),

Chalna, Goalundo, and Jamalpur can be mentioned as places of distinct promise.

Before we describe our principal towns, we should understand that the close massing of people together in towns and cities is not a simple matter. It calls for special plans and arrangements. Such things as sanitation, medical relief, food supply, security, transport, education, and housing cannot be left to chance. Our older cities, like Lahore, are too crowded to be really desirable places in which to live unless improvements are carried out. Those who built the old walled city of Lahore had very little knowledge about health. They were so concerned with making it into a strong fortress against armed enemies that they entirely forgot to give it any open spaces. They provided only narrow roads and lanes, with tall houses shutting out the health-giving sunlight and fresh air. It is only outside the walled city that we find better conditions, in the splendid suburbs which now lie north, east, and south of Lahore.

Similarly, Peshawar, Hyderabad (Sind), Dacca, and some of our old walled towns were badly arranged when first built. When epidemic diseases broke out, they became dangerous places in which to live. Nowadays we have better ideas. The old towns were badly designed because the rulers of those times did not know much about the needs of the people. The rulers or their viceroys or governors, long before the coming of the British, constructed many beautiful buildings, but they lived in palaces or garden houses far from the towns, and visited the latter only for official purposes. The citizens were equally ignorant, and had no voice in the management or lay-out of their towns.

The people who are naturally the most interested in

their surroundings are those who have to stay there all their lives. They are born and brought up there, do their daily work there, and make their homes there. Almost everything that happens in the town affects them in some way. In the villages there are *panchayats* which act for the well-being of the village folk. It is more difficult, however, to make the best arrangements for the tens of thousands of people who live in a town.

When the British began to rule northern India, they noticed that the citizens at that time were taking very little part in the management of the towns. They wished to encourage the townspeople to show greater interest and help to make their towns better places in which to live. They therefore set up 'municipalities', which were comprised of official members (appointed by the Government) and elected members chosen by the citizens. These municipalities were given the task of making by-laws on everything that concerned the well-being of the town; they also had to see to the carrying out of their orders by the officers and servants of the municipality.

Although this system of town management was not completely successful, it gave the citizens a better chance to make their wishes known, and it increased their pride in their towns. They could tell their municipal representatives to give them a purer water supply, more water pipes, underground drainage, bigger parks and recreation grounds, more hospitals, better roads, more schools, cleaner market-places, healthier dwelling-houses, children's playgrounds, public libraries, and many other improvements.

There is nothing unusual in this method of asking townspeople to take a share in the management of their local affairs. All modern countries have that system. The mighty cities of London, New York, Paris, Amsterdam, Ankara, Cairo, Rome, Brussels, and many others have their own City Corporations; the smaller cities and large towns all over the world have their 'municipal councils'. The Central or State Governments seldom interfere, although they have the right to control. 'Local self-government' is one of the best ways in which 'democracy' works. The municipalities hold their own meetings and debates, and are a good means of training public-spirited men for a country's parliaments and for civic responsibilities.

In Pakistan so many strange and difficult problems arose in the first three years of our country's existence that it is not surprising that our municipalities are not yet playing their full part in public life. For example, the great crowds of refugees who in 1947 flocked into Karachi (our biggest city) upset all the ordinary arrangements there. The Central Government therefore at once took over the management of Karachi and for the time being the old Municipal Corporation has been disbanded. When conditions become more favourable, it will probably be restored.

A little over a hundred years ago Karachi was nothing more than a tiny fishing town of 'low mud hovels and tall mud houses with flat mud roofs'. To-day nearly 1,500,000 people live in the vast city which has sprung up, covering nearly eighty square miles with many suburbs on the north, west, and east sides. The 'mud huts' have been transformed into handsome stone and brick houses. Next only to New Delhi, Karachi is the grandest and most dignified city between Cairo and Singapore. In population it rivals both Bombay and Calcutta. As a seaport it is nearly as important as Colombo. It is easily Asia's greatest airport.

The British first landed at Karachi in 1843. They saw that it had a good natural harbour and that it occupied an important strategic position at the northern head of the Arabian Sea. From Karachi their battleships commanded the ocean to the Persian Gulf in the west and Ceylon in the south and the whole of the Bombay coast, as well as the east coast of Africa. After the making of the Suez Canal, Karachi was 200 miles nearer to England than was Bombay. With the dawn of the Era of Flight, it is the first point at which aeroplanes call at the Indo-Pakistan sub-continent on their way from Europe. North of Karachi stretches 1,000 miles of Western Pakistan, to which this port is the only real gateway.

The British soon began to develop the tiny fishing town. They built a naval harbour there, and for the next sixty years kept on improving it, until in 1907 it was declared to be a 'first-class port'. During both World Wars a great deal of new trade came to Karachi. Meanwhile, it had long been connected by railway with the Punjab and Delhi, and with Central India, Surat, and Bombay. By the year 1947 its population was estimated at 425,000, and its total annual trade had risen to well over 52 crores of rupees.

The Partition brought about a tremendous change in the life of Karachi. Up to 1947 so many Hindus had come to live and trade there that in the city itself they outnumbered the Muslims, although Sind Province as a whole had a very large Muslim majority. As soon as Pakistan was created, the Hindus suddenly went back to Bharat, and in their place came a stream of Muslim refugees from Bombay, Gujarat, Cutch, Kathiawar, and the Deccan, and from East Punjab, Delhi, the United

Provinces, and Bihar. About a million of these Muhajireens poured into Karachi. They overflowed from the city into emergency camps.

The unexpected arrival of such numbers created many problems. They had to be given food, which fortunately was plentiful. The water supply had to be increased at once. Every care had to be taken to prevent sickness. As a large proportion of the refugees have remained permanently, work has had to be arranged for them. Tens of thousands of new houses are being built. A 'Greater Karachi' is being planned, with new roads, new suburbs and new parks, with more buses and tram routes, as well as a circular railway.

In addition, Karachi has become the capital of the whole of our country. Our Governor-General lives here. Here is the Federal Assembly. Here are the Embassies of over twenty-five countries. Here are the offices of numerous business firms. At Drigh Road (close to Karachi) is Asia's biggest airport, with its great buildings and aviation training schools. One of Karachi's new suburbs will take the form of a huge 'Industrial Trading Estate', covering 2,000 acres, where 500 big and small factories will be built to give work to a lakh of labourers. About fifty-four villages will be taken into Greater Karachi, which will cover 566 square miles of land—nearly as large an area as Greater London.

All this cannot be done in a day. The work will occupy some years. It means a gigantic effort. But eventually Karachi will be one of the most splendid cities in the East, with well-planned and well-built business and residential quarters, its own university town and large naval and air headquarters. Its docks, which already hold 500 ships a year, will be improved so as to give anchorage to many more. In 1949-50, the port's trade was nearly three million tons of goods.

What Karachi is to Western Pakistan, Chittagong is to Eastern Bengal. Although not nearly so large a city, and not overflooded with refugees, it can well become as great a seaport. Situated near the mouth of a large river, it has a splendid natural harbour which very big ships can safely use. It commands the Bay of Bengal and the Indian Ocean down to Singapore and Ceylon. Its trade is with all the countries of the East and also with Europe, America, and Australia.

Unfortunately, Chittagong was a port neglected for many years under British rule, and when it was given to Pakistan in 1947, the wharves were in a bad condition caused by over-usage in the 1939-45 World War. Its history starts much earlier than Karachi's. It was well known to the Arab sailors of 800 years ago. In 1538 the Portuguese burnt the town in revenge for the imprisonment of their envoys. In 1582 it became a separate district under Moghal rule. Nearly 100 years later Shaista Khan, then Moghal Governor of Bengal, defeated the Portuguese pirates there and changed the name of the port to Islamabad. Chittagong was handed over to the East India Company in 1760 by Nawab Mir Kasim, after the Battle of Plassey. Its trade revived, but the rise of Calcutta as a port forced Chittagong into second place, and 150 years passed before it regained some of its former trade.

It was the opening of the Assam-Bengal Railway in 1895 that brought new prosperity to Chittagong, for the railway carried much of the trade in rice, jute, and tea there. It was declared a major port in 1928. Much use of it was made in landing troops and munitions during the campaigns of 1943-5 to drive the Japanese out of Burma.

Since the creation of Pakistan, Chittagong has come strongly to the front, and is now a serious rival to Calcutta. Much of the tea and jute which formerly went to Calcutta from Sylhet and Eastern Bengal is now sent to Chittagong for export direct to other parts of the world. Here arrive big cargoes of coal and cloth from abroad. A vast new programme has been drawn up to construct new jetties, erect new machinery, and improve the railway yards. Jute and other factories will also be built. In 1947 the port had a trade of one million tons; by 1950 this had increased to $2\frac{1}{2}$ million tons per annum. The total value of exports and imports is over Rs. 55 crores a year.

So quick has been Chittagong's rise that a plan has been made to construct another great seaport at Chalna, in Khulna district, not far away, where a good harbour has been found. This town is on the Pussar River, one of the mouths of the Meghna. Work has begun on this scheme, which will cost Rs. 145 millions, and be completed by the year 1953. The new port of Chalna will provide eight berths for cargo vessels, with the necessary sheds and warehouses, railways, roads, bridges, and cranes. This will relieve the heavy burden now falling on Chittagong.

Dacca, although far from the sea, is an inland trading centre of great importance as well as the capital of Eastern Pakistan. Its history has already been traced in an earlier chapter of this book. The creation of Pakistan has brought new life and hope to this city of 300,000 inhabitants. Its industrious and clever artisans have naturally attracted to Dacca many of our leading industrialists, who are setting up cotton and jute factories so as to be independent of supplies from Bharat.

As in the case of Karachi, though to a much smaller extent, Dacca received a large number of refugees and new-comers. This created a housing problem which is being scientifically solved by expert architects and engineers. The city is being expanded and improved. Its older narrow streets and crowded houses are being replaced by wide avenues and well-planned dwellings, with many parks and recreation grounds. Water supply and drainage are being introduced. The streets are to be lighted with electricity instead of kerosene lamps. Above all else, a ceaseless war is being waged against dirt, disease, and squalor. Malaria, from which its people formerly suffered severely, has been completely stamped out through the extermination of the Anopheles mosquito. A fine new city of Dacca, more worthy of its place as a provincial capital, is rapidly being created.

CHAPTER XVII

LIFE AT SCHOOL AND COLLEGE

What a joy it is for a young person to go to school or college. There the pupil, whether boy or girl, attends classes happily with companions of the same age and takes part, not only in lessons, but in healthy games. All the time, too, there is the satisfaction of knowing that he or she is gaining in knowledge and experience which will some day be of great use to our country and to our fellow-beings all over the world.

We do not live for our selfish interests alone. Our lives are made up of 'give' as well as 'take'. We owe our comfortable homes and the necessaries of life to our parents and friends. Around us we see people busy with their work and professions. They earn incomes with which they support their families, and at the same time their occupations are valuable to our Pakistan. We in our turn look forward to the day when we will become useful citizens. Then we will be the 'givers'—giving help to our relatives and strength to our country.

We will have our jobs. Some of us will become careful farmers; others will make goods of all kinds; others will take part in the protection of our country by joining the Armed Forces. Many different forms of usefulness lie before us, as doctors, teachers, engineers, lawyers, bankers, accountants, clerks, businessmen, traders, factory managers, foresters, transport workers, airmen, telegraphists, merchant seamen, weavers, livestock breeders,

Government officials. There are hundreds of different occupations from which each of us can make his or her choice.

Whatever happens to be the line of work awaiting us, each young person is eager to do well in it and to be thought well of by his friends. We certainly would not care to be regarded as idlers, who are a burden to a country and who give nothing to its welfare. Nor would we like to contribute anything but our best efforts.

How well we do in life depends upon the knowledge and ambition we gain in our school and college days. Looking around us, we can see everywhere that the knowledge and skill acquired by other people have helped to make our own lives more pleasant and convenient. If we live in a comfortable house, we can admire the cleverness of the architect who designed it and the patient labour of those who made the brickwork and fitted the doors and windows so neatly. We travel by car or train or aeroplane, and wonder at the scientific skill of those who planned and made every detail of such powerful machines. We can realize when watching a cinema or listening to the wireless what a great amount of study and research must have been carried out in producing such inventions. We listen to a sermon in a mosque, and are astonished at the learning and wisdom shown by the preacher. And so it is with everything in our lives. Nothing is achieved without learning. Civilization is built up on the lessons of childhood and college days.

Long ago, before history was written, men were already learning. Their fathers and mothers were the teachers; they still are the first teachers. From early childhood they show us how to walk and dress, to do things for ourselves, and to speak. We begin our education in our infancy. Even animals teach their young how to do simple things—how to hunt and how to defend themselves. But, whereas animals are able to reason only slightly, man has a wonderful brain which is able to understand many things. He has a great power of memory and of connecting facts with each other in such a way as to create more knowledge. He can count and he can imagine. He is able to draw designs which have a meaning. Although he cannot predict the future, he can make plans, because he knows from experience what is most likely to happen.

The building up of such knowledge takes time. The quantity of such knowledge also is always increasing. Let us think how much more we have to learn to-day than did, for example, the people of the Indus Valley civilization four thousand years ago, or the wild jungle folk who inhabited the earth long before them. Even in those early times they knew how to make signs and talk to each other. At first they could tell each other strange stories of the daily happenings in their lives. Those who heard those stories would recount them to their children, and these would remember and relate them to the next generation. When man became more civilized and invented written signs for the language he spoke, it became easier to spread knowledge and to make knowledge permanent. Bit by bit all this knowledge has increased, until to-day we can work out difficult problems in mathematics and science or write books full of scholarship and wisdom.

Unfortunately, because modern civilization has not spread evenly over the face of the earth, there are still many people who do not share with us the boon of education. This does not mean that they learn nothing. It means, however, that they learn only by word of mouth what their parents can tell them about the simplest things in their lives. Not being taught how to read and write, they cannot become as useful and wise as they could be. Many naturally clever people thus have no chance of making the best use of their talents. They are forced to lead the simplest and poorest of lives, and their country loses what could be very valuable service.

In Pakistan to-day, it is sad for us to find that nine out of ten of our men, women, and children cannot read or write. This, of course, does not mean that they are completely ignorant. They do, in fact, know a good deal about their crops or their other ways of earning a living. If only they could read simple books, their knowledge would be greatly increased, and they would be able to lead healthier and more useful lives. They would know better how to do their daily work and how to avoid things that are likely to harm them. They would thus become more efficient citizens.

It is the great wish and hope of all wise men in Pakistan that every single man and woman should be a good citizen, giving of his or her best to our country's welfare. We want their minds to grow, as well as their bodies. With the help of education our peasants and our artisans can become far more productive workers. Their curiosity will be aroused, and the more they learn the more they will wish to learn. There is so much knowledge awaiting them, by which they will be able to make better use of their fields or their implements. As a race our people are gifted with a high level of reason and intelligence, and even the poorest among them can rise to true greatness.

So far, unfortunately, it has not been possible to educate more than a small proportion of our people.

Schools cost money for buildings, furniture, books, and teachers. Under British rule some progress was made, but not nearly enough. Independent Pakistan is determined to do better than that. The aim is to bring education within the reach of every child, and thereby to give him the first right to which a citizen is entitled—the gift of knowledge, the banishment of ignorance.

The total number of boys and girls of school-going age in Pakistan is at least five millions, but at present about four millions do not go to school. Our Government has decided that by degrees primary education will be made free and compulsory for all children between the ages of 6 and 14 years. This will be a very great task to carry out, and cannot be completed without careful planning spread over several years. It means the building of tens of thousands of new schools all over Pakistan, until every village and town possesses its own school-houses. Enormous sums of money will have to be set aside by the Government for the construction of such buildings and for the training and salaries of the lakhs of teachers who will be needed. When every child is being taught, the total cost of Primary Education will be Rs. 400 millions per annum only for the running of the schools. A beginning has already been made with the scheme for universal compulsory free education.

Is it worth our while to spend such a large sum? Who is there that would say 'No'? Money has been poured out on our irrigation canals. It has been amply repaid by the rich crops that can now grow on what were lately desert tracts. Canal water has brought fertility to our fields. Education will bring fertility into the minds of our people. Then everything that they undertake will be done in better and wiser ways, because they will know how to think and to reason. They will have the knowledge with which to make the work of their hands more productive. They will be able to plan and to understand the use of labour-saving devices, such as machinery in their fields, in their houses and industries, and in the transport of their products.

Education, however, is desirable not merely for its usefulness. There are other boons which it confers on the people. Indeed, the first influence which it has on the minds of its recipients is the way it enables them to share in the practice of their religion. As an Islamic land we attach the highest importance to the proper service of God. The person who can read the Holy Quran and our other sacred writings is far better able to carry out his religious observances. Into his life comes spirituality, so that his daily actions are governed by virtue and not by mere selfish motives.

It is also part of our Islamic way of life that we should treat the non-Muslim members of our nation with tolerance, equality, and social justice. We have promised to let them enjoy their religious liberties. With the spread of education all our people will find it easier to understand each other and serve their country and their fellow-beings to the best of their abilities.

Education is something more than a mere matter of reading, writing, and arithmetic. It aims at improving all three of the elements in man—his mind, his body, and his moral qualities. The books which a child studies at school help him to increase his knowledge and to use his brains. Outside the classroom he learns to exercise his muscles, and grow strong and healthy. His religious training and the way he learns to exercise self-control, develop his moral sense and teach him the right rules of behaviour, so that he remains a just and honest person all his life. He learns to see all sides of a question. He learns to love peace for its own sake. He becomes a good influence among his neighbours. Above all else, he grows up to be a God-fearing man. Those are qualities which Pakistanis cherish and which help to make a nation great.

For many young people it is desirable that education should not stop at the Primary stage, but continue for at least three or four years longer. Between the ages of 13 and 18 the mind is still able to take in fresh knowledge without great effort. This is the Secondary stage of education. To those who benefit by it, the country will look for the lakhs of teachers and instructors required and also for large numbers of more highly skilled workers in agriculture, industry, and commerce. This will be the very useful class of people who will occupy the middle grades and be able to train the humbler workers in farm, factory, or office. They will be of great value as supervisors, because their knowledge and experience will teach them a sense of initiative and responsibility.

From this it is evident that Secondary Education is really divided into two natural compartments—the general literary subjects, such as language, history, geography, citizenship, mathematics, and science, with some instruction in handwork; and Vocational Training in handicraft arts, such as carpentry, smithery, agriculture, spinning, weaving, bookbinding, printing, leatherwork, tailoring, sewing, drawing, music, gardening, and cooking —with some instruction in language, history, geography, mathematics, and science. According to his personal tastes and ability, each pupil will be able to follow the course that seems preferable. In this way he will be usefully and happily occupied, and at the end of his

Secondary School career he will be able to find suitable work in which he can do himself full justice.

The setting up of more Secondary Schools, both General and Technical, is one of the aims of our Government, and various schemes have been prepared. Some of our industrialists are also eager to help, especially in the training of skilled technical workers and supervisors. They are able to take apprentices, who learn the more advanced and complicated processes in factories, mines, laboratories, and offices, and afterwards become expert supervisors and instructors.

A further step planned is two-year Higher Secondary courses for students aged 18 and 19, which will give better qualifications to those who have completed the Secondary stage. The courses will include both general subjects and a wide range of technical and commercial subjects, giving ambitious young people an opportunity to specialize.

Then will follow the various Honours Graduation Degree courses (three years for the B.A., one further year for the M.A., and yet one year longer for the Doctor's degree) which will enable students to obtain the highest qualifications in Arts, Science, Engineering, Divinity, Commerce, Education, Agriculture, and Medicine and Surgery. Those who pass through the universities will be chosen for the higher positions in their professions.

There are already good universities at Lahore, Dacca, and Karachi. One more is also being created at Peshawar for the N.W.F.P. These universities offer courses in all the subjects mentioned in the last paragraph. They are staffed by professors, lecturers, and demonstrators, who have high qualifications. The colleges forming part of the universities are to be found in all our chief towns. They are well provided with hostels, gymnasia, and sports fields. Their degrees are recognized by universities all over the world. Several thousand students (including women, for whom in some cases there are separate colleges) attend our university courses.

Because our colleges are not yet able in some cases to give complete up-to-date instruction, especially in very advanced or highly technical subjects, some of our most promising students are given State Scholarships to attend foreign universities. There are about 650 Pakistanis, both men and women, studying in the United Kingdom, and considerable numbers have also gone to the United States. Many of them have been admitted into British or American factories, mines, banks, and commercial offices, where they learn the most modern methods of production and business. Some have gone there at their own expense. Among the State scholars (who receive sufficient grants of money from the Pakistan Government) are medical students, nurses, engineers, teachers, scientists, and technicians. On returning to Pakistan, these teach their new knowledge to others and help to plan and equip our factories.

From early childhood until the highest stage, therefore, our young people are being encouraged to make the best possible use of the many educational opportunities offered to them. All the work is under the control of the Department of Education in each province. To make sure that our schools and colleges are well staffed and equipped, given sufficient grants of money and properly managed, the Department sends its own inspectors to visit them. New ways are always tried to make the lessons and courses more interesting and useful. Our radio gives special broadcasts to help the teachers and instruct the pupils.

Some of the schools have their own cinema or lantern-slide projectors.

While all this is being done for our young students, our older people have not been forgotten. Many grown-up men and women are sorry that they were not taught to read and write in their childhood. Our Government is helping them by setting up Adult Schools, which are becoming popular in the towns and villages. No person is ever too old to learn, and there is no limit to what we can learn. Our country is the gainer.

Top: In Pakistan reaping by hand is slow.

Below: A 'combine harvester' reaps, threshes and loads the grain in one operation.

Top: It takes this man twenty minutes to saw through a log.

Below: An electric circular saw can do the same work in a few seconds.

CHAPTER XVIII

HEALTH AND STRENGTH

NATURE has blessed the average Pakistani with a strong body. As a nation we have nothing to be ashamed of in our physique. We are descended from vigorous races, who were accustomed to the hardships of emigration and warfare. Our early ancestors, both Aryans and Moghals, came from the cold Central Asiatic highlands, where the climate hardens men's frames. In stature our people compare on equal terms with the sturdiest nations on earth. Whether in Eastern or Western Pakistan, our peasants can work untiringly in the hottest or coldest of weather and our labourers have great powers of endurance—so long as they are able to obtain sufficient food and so long as simple precautions are taken to protect their health.

In this respect there is not much difference between Western and Eastern Pakistan. In the north-west our people are as a rule of bigger build than their fellow-countrymen in Eastern Bengal. That, however, is due only to climatic causes. In the same way we find that Englishmen from the northern counties are taller and broader-boned than the Londoner; yet in courage, determination, and endurance the two are fully equal. Our Chittagong seamen are splendid specimens of humanity. Our Baluchis and frontiersmen are sometimes of gigantic build. Western Punjab has bred sons of prodigious strength. Many *pahlwans* too have belonged to Eastern Bengal families. All are equally courageous.

Unfortunately, in the last few generations many causes have arisen to harm the health of our population and weaken their vitality. In an earlier chapter we mentioned the three dreaded diseases of plague, cholera, and malaria, and we described the methods by which these could be kept in check and finally beaten. There are other serious diseases which we also need to examine. Not least among these is tuberculosis. Smallpox is a horrible danger. Dysentery and typhoid take heavy toll of life everywhere. In parts of Eastern Bengal there are constant outbreaks of kala-azar, beriberi, and hookworm disease. Added to this list are other ailments which, although not so dangerous to life, harm the efficiency of the sufferer and make him only too often a helpless burden to his relations. These troubles include widespread diseases of the eyes, leading to blindness or impaired eyesight. Far too many infants die before they complete their first year of life. Far too many mothers also die in childbirth.

Before we consider how such ills can be cured, we should not fail to notice that they occur less heavily where the people are well nourished and where homes and surroundings are kept thoroughly clean. Disease and death always lurk where there is dirt or hunger. The microbes which cause disease cannot breed if filthy pools and refuse heaps are never tolerated. Germs hate sunshine. Strict sanitation is therefore the first and most effective weapon with which we must fight disease. 'Prevention is better than cure' should be the watchword of every person in village, town, or city. Each one of the diseases we have already mentioned is directly spread by disobeying the laws of sanitation.

The first people to fall victims to disease are those whose

bodies have already been weakened by lack of sufficient food. Their natural resistance to sickness is lowered. Their blood is too thin to fight the microbes, and the sufferer's life is soon endangered. That is why great famines in olden days were usually followed by widespread epidemics of cholera, enteric, and dysentery. In modern times famine conditions can be quickly relieved by sending trainloads of food to the districts concerned. Even so, as perhaps some of us remember, there was a great shortage of rice and pulses in Bengal during 1946-7, just before the Partition. Because of the 1939-45 World War, not enough rice had been grown in Burma, Siam, Malaya, and the Dutch East Indies for any to be spared for Bengal. We still largely depend on good monsoons for our food crops. Scarcity of food is therefore still to be guarded against. One of our first concerns must be to increase our food supply and to build up reserve stocks of grain so that our people will always have enough to eat.

We cannot feel contented even with those words 'enough to eat'. To be really vigorous and healthy—able to resist disease—our people must have not merely quantities of food, but meals which contain enough nourishment. In this scientific age we know that the different 'vitamins' help us to grow and to keep in good health. A limited and monotonous diet does not provide sufficient vitamins, which are the life-giving elements in food. Children, for example, need plenty of milk and vegetables. Fish, too, is rich in body-building properties. Large numbers of our people are unable to take enough of these better varieties of nourishment because they cannot afford to buy them. Our Government is trying hard to remedy this by encouraging better agriculture and industries, so that the people can earn larger incomes through increased production, and thus have more money to spare for food.

One by one the obstacles to preserving the health of the nation are thus being removed. It is not a task only for a handful of Government doctors and other officials. 'Prevention' is something in which every man, woman, or child can co-operate. Nobody would deliberately refuse to help. Great numbers, however, still fail to co-operate, because either they are careless or they have not yet had their eyes opened. It is for the educated classes ceaselessly to keep on instructing those who are still ignorant about such matters.

Every schoolchild can become a valuable helper in this national health campaign. Every boy or girl who reads this chapter can make up his or her mind to set a good example. What they can make sure of is that they allow no heaps of decaying rubbish to pile up near their houses, and no stagnant water to collect in drains or pools. The older people can insist upon their towns being kept clean and wholesome by the local municipalities. The *panchayats* can make arrangements with the villagers to see that the advice given by sanitary inspectors is carried out by one and all. When there are no more breeding-places for microbes, flies, mosquitoes, and other dangerous creatures, there will be far less chance of epidemics breaking out.

If, in spite of all such precautions, by some unlucky accident an epidemic does happen to occur, it is then the duty of every person to co-operate in making sure that the disease spreads no farther. The Government in such cases has its plans ready immediately to deal with the situation. While its preventive measures are being put into operation, the people can help by keeping calm and

HEALTH AND STRENGTH

readily obeying the instructions given them. The first care is to take the sick to isolation hospitals, where they will be given proper medicines and nursed back to health without fear of spreading the disease to others. The most foolish action of all is for a person to give way to panic and try to run away; by doing so he may be only carrying the infection to new places and causing much harm there. The Health Department workers can be depended upon to know their job, and an outbreak of disease can be checked and confined to one place. Meanwhile, the general public can take such simple precautions as submitting to inoculation or vaccination, drinking only boiled water, eating only cooked food, avoiding crowded places, and removing any rubbish dumps. When the wisdom of 'Prevention' is understood by all, epidemics will become rare in town and village alike. 'Prevention' comes best from 'cleanliness'.

Quite apart from epidemics, all human beings are liable to fall ill or to meet with accidents. These are 'acts of God', and ordinary human precautions cannot always prevent them. It is then that we turn to our doctors, our nurses, and our hospitals for a cure. To provide them in sufficient numbers has called for very great efforts on the part of our Government. The first three years of its existence found Pakistan faced with immense difficulties, because at the 1947 Partition many doctors and nurses left the country, causing a serious shortage here, while the movements of millions of refugees added to the confusion and danger.

To make matters still more difficult, several important places like the Central Research Institute at Kasauli, the All-India Institute of Public Health at Calcutta, the Malaria Institute of India, the Central Drugs Laboratory at Calcutta, and the College of Nursing all went over to Bharat. Pakistan had to make plans to set up similar institutions of its own. Steps had to be taken also to train new doctors. As the medical course covers at least five years, it will take time before we have enough doctors for our country's needs. Medicine is a highly skilled profession and requires advanced studies. To make sure that our doctors will be of the best quality, eighteen to twenty medical graduates are being sent as State scholars to London and New York annually to take higher degrees. When they return, they will be able to teach our younger medical students as well as to attend hospital patients.

The shortage of nurses was even more serious than that of doctors when Pakistan was created. The proper running of hospitals and the care of the sick depend very largely on a sufficiency of nurses. In addition, the country was in great need of Health Visitors. Our Government quickly laid plans to train more nurses, and sent the first batch to study more advanced nursing in the United Kingdom. Meanwhile, Pakistan is setting up three Nurses' Training Schools (at Karachi, Lahore, and Dacca), where 120 women and girls annually will be taught this most useful of all professions.

Another important step has been the establishment of the Fatima Jinnah Medical College for Women at Lahore, where fifty students will be admitted annually for the five-year degree course in Medicine and Surgery. It is the first college of its kind in Pakistan. Its graduates have a career of great dignity and usefulness opened to them, for the proper medical treatment of women is one of the most essential services. A nation consists of women as well as of men, and the health of the former is perhaps the most important concern in the life of a country. In

Pakistan, Welfare Centres and Clinics for Mothers and Children are being established at many centres. All lives are of equal value where the well-being and general fitness of our nation is concerned. This has been recognized in the daily supply of free milk which is being issued to refugee children at various refugee centres throughout Pakistan under a United Nations Scheme to which our Government gives its help. Nearly every district of Pakistan to-day has a Women's Hospital and Children's Clinic, and more of these are being built.

The preservation of a nation's health requires more arrangements even than the provision of hospitals, doctors, and nurses in sufficient numbers or of health inspectors and sanitation squads. Ceaseless study of the causes and nature of diseases has to be carried on at all times, and preventive measures have to be kept in preparation. For this there are research institutions and laboratories, some of which concentrate on particular diseases. At the laboratories are made the various vaccines and serums which are required for the prevention or treatment of ailments. The laboratories also manufacture many kinds of pure drugs and medicines required for hospital use. These tasks are under the general guidance of the newly created Pakistan Medical Research Association.

Special efforts are being made to drive malaria and tuberculosis out of our land, and these are meeting with success in Baluchistan, the N.W.F.P., Sind, Mymensingh, and elsewhere. Malaria has already been driven out of Dacca. Doctors are also working hard to show how people can be vaccinated against tuberculosis. A very great deal, however, remains to be done before we can say that disease and sickness are conquered in Pakistan.

Apart from fighting diseases within our boundaries, our Government also keeps watch on the seaports and airports, so as to prevent infection from entering or leaving Pakistan by ship or by aeroplane. Our country is also a member of the World Health Organization and the United Nations Organization, which has been helping us in our anti-disease war.

As a further precaution we have laws to make sure that only pure drugs and medicines can be sold to the public. There are also laws to prevent the adulteration of food; people who mix injurious substances in our ghee, milk, or oil or other articles of food are liable to punishment. As we grow older we too can help to bring about many other health reforms. Public opinion now condemns shops that sell meat, fish, or vegetables which are exposed to dust, flies, and germs. It is also very harmful for people to eat fruit which has been cut or damaged by bad plucking or packing, for disease germs then easily enter the fruit through the torn peels. Contaminated meat and fruit spread sicknesses such as cholera, dysentery, and typhoid.

It is a great consolation to us to realize that year by year our own lives and those of our dear ones will become safer through the ceaseless war against disease. Both 'prevention' and 'cure' will become more easily procurable through the improvements in sanitation, hospitals, nursing, and medical attendance. Each boy and girl can help to hasten this general improvement by spreading the good knowledge we have gained. We should never hesitate to express our horror and disgust when we behold the laws of health broken by the careless actions of others. We should fearlessly explain to the ignorant the dangerous results of failure to keep our towns and villages

HEALTH AND STRENGTH

clean. We cannot all become doctors or nurses, but each of us can become a guardian of the public health.

In our lives, too, we can make sure of escaping disease by taking the same precautions ourselves. Cleanliness, good food, pure water, and sunlight—these are our four safeguards. By taking part in games and exercises, too, we can help to keep our own bodies fit and well. We can join the Pakistan Red Cross Society and the St. John Ambulance Association of Pakistan, both of which train us in simple nursing, first-aid, and healthy living. Our Girl Guide and Boy Scout Associations also do a great deal to improve our knowledge of sanitation and hygiene. Through all these means each of us can promote the ideal of 'a healthy mind in a healthy body', which is as true of a nation as of an individual.

CHAPTER XIX

SPORT AND GOOD SPORTSMANSHIP

In any scheme of 'Keep-fit' for the nation, sport deserves to be given high prominence. It is an essential part of every young Pakistani's education, and one which nearly all boys and girls and college students thoroughly enjoy. It is extremely popular throughout our country's Armed Forces, in whose training it has a daily place. Large numbers of the general population also exhibit the keenest interest, as is shown by the crowds that assemble to watch hockey, cricket, football, or lawn tennis matches, or displays of boxing, wrestling, swimming, and athletics, in both Eastern and Western Pakistan. Apart from the 'Western' sports, we have many village games which have been handed down to us for generations. Pakistan is indeed a sports-loving country.

It is only natural that this should be the case, for our people are blessed with inherited vigour and a keen interest in activity. They have a wish to make good and healthy use of their leisure and energy. Sport thus makes an immense appeal to their instinctive tastes. Perhaps it is a survival of primitive man's early emotions; hunting used to stimulate his sense of fitness and bring him the joy of a successful chase in which he and his companions excelled. Or it may be an inclination produced by the old warlike traditions of our nearer ancestors.

Whatever be the reasons, Pakistanis to-day have a widespread love for games and sport and do extremely

SPORT AND GOOD SPORTSMANSHIP 153

well at these. From the point of view of physical fitness, the exercise gained in a person's young days is of lasting value. The bodily frame is built up and hardened; the muscles are developed, and one's movements become co-ordinated, while sight and hearing are made more acute. Moreover, especially for the student who has to spend long hours at his desk, games bring necessary relief and variety into the daily routine. The mind becomes freshened even while the body is strengthened. Education's threefold aim, as we have already remarked, is to develop the mind, the body, and the moral spirit of an individual so as to make him a completely useful citizen. Sport and games help this process, because they train all three of those qualities.

Besides sharpening the player's intelligence, most games are an excellent means of cultivating a person's character. At cricket, football, hockey, and tennis, as well as in other forms of sport, the player often has to make up his mind quickly. This develops the habit of decisiveness. Perseverance is also strengthened, together with determination not to give in, but to keep on trying to the last. At the same time a person learns to respect his opponent. Whether winning or losing, it is the effort that counts even more than the result. We are not all equal in skill or strength, and nobody can win every time. The really important thing is whether a man or woman can hold his or her head up bravely and say, 'I tried my best'. That same spirit will show itself in daily life and help a person to become a well-respected citizen.

In addition, the 'rules of the game' teach a person respect for law and order in general. He learns that if the rules are broken, the offender is penalized: at cricket the batsman is given 'out', or the bowler gives away a run by sending down a 'no-ball'; at football or hockey the referee awards a free kick or a free hit to the opponents if a player is 'offside' or plays roughly. Similarly, a person learns to obey the laws of his country and helps to see that others obey them too. Games thus help to develop the sense of 'right and wrong' and of 'fair play', which is also of the greatest value in ordinary dealings in life.

This is true, not only of the actual 'letter of the law', but equally of the moral attitude. There is such a thing as 'the spirit of the game'—which means the right way in which it is played. We often hear the expression, 'It isn't cricket'. Those words signify that some action, even if not positively wrong, is not agreeable to others, or that it reveals some meanness in the mind of the doer.

The true sportsman never stoops to petty or spiteful tricks by which he could derive an unfair advantage over others. He 'plays fair' and is open and honest in his movements. In a race he does not deliberately obstruct a rival or dig his elbows into a runner who is overtaking him. At football he does not slyly kick an opponent on the ankle in order to injure him. Nor at hockey does he purposely trip a player, while pretending to be trying to hit the ball. The true sportsman detests such 'low tactics', and prefers to play the game in the proper gentlemanly spirit. It is better to lose playing fairly than to win by questionable methods. The genuine sportsman is liked by all and makes many friends, because they know he is to be trusted. Similarly, we can be looked upon as 'good sportsmen' in the everyday affairs of business and public life.

Most modern games are team games, in which the result depends upon the combined efforts of several players.

Even lawn tennis has its 'doubles', in which partners have to play together. The stronger and better players help the weaker and less skilful members of their side, and the idea of co-operation is cultivated in all of them. Their passing, their covering of each other's movements, their dash to a comrade's rescue when they find him in a difficult position or overworked, their obedience to the captain's orders (even if this means some personal inconvenience to themselves)—all these foster co-operation and a sense of mutual dependence. A respect for the referee's decisions teaches the quality of respect for the laws of the land and a sense of justice.

At the same time, by this free co-operation they voluntarily submit themselves to a common discipline, which signifies the subordination of the individual for the sake of the good of the whole team. Much the same is required of them in the affairs of ordinary life. In business or official work, there is little room for the entirely selfish individual. The self-seeker is soon found out by others, and never really gains the confidence of his colleagues, because they know full well that he is striving only for his personal gain and not for a common cause. Team work does not mean, of course, that a player must not use his own judgment and initiative; it does, however, ensure that his motive is to help his team-mates rather than to make a hero of himself.

With traditions of fair play, chivalry, and co-operation already well-established as their Code of Honour—as is only natural in the case of an Islamic nation—Pakistanis took happily to Western sport when it was introduced by the British during the second half of the last century. The traditional English games of cricket and football were played here first by the officers and soldiers of the

British Army when they were stationed in cantonments all over the Punjab and the North-West Frontier, and by a few English civilians. They introduced these games into the Indian Army units and into the colleges, who took them up readily.

Polo had rapidly become popular among cavalry officers, and many of our horsemen soon showed great skill at this game—as was to be expected of a race who were (and are) grand riders. Moreover, polo of a kind used to be played in Moghal days, though the modern rules of that game were not decided until about 1880.

Hockey had become a favourite game in the public schools and universities of England by the end of the last century and quickly spread to our own colleges, where the students showed brilliant skill—which has made Pakistan hockey famous in the world of to-day. Meanwhile, lawn tennis also had begun to capture the public fancy. Badminton, developed at Poona, was another active game which gave our young people opportunities for exercise and rivalry. Golf, on the other hand, never obtained a hold in our country, chiefly because it required courses which are expensive to make and maintain in good condition. Volley-ball and basket-ball offer splendid exercise.

It was early in this century that sport became a universal interest in the regions that are now Eastern and Western Pakistan. Games increasingly formed part of the recognized activities of schools and colleges, and annual athletic sports were regularly organized. Senior officials and businessmen of all communities gave useful encouragement by offering handsome cups, shields, and medals as trophies. This resulted in the formation of numerous leagues and tournaments for all the more popular games, so that the spirit of rivalry was awakened. Perhaps there are too many such competitions.

In order to control and supervise them, each major sport organized its own provincial association. Later these joined together to form All-India Football, Hockey, Polo, and Lawn Tennis Federations, an All-India Board of Cricket Control, and similar central governing bodies for boxing, swimming, cycling, and athletics. These drew up the general rules for the competitions, and were managed by councils and committees containing representatives elected by the provincial associations. The various clubs who were members of these provincial associations also had the right to vote for the provincial committees and district committees. In this way each branch of sport conducted its own affairs on democratic lines. Generally speaking, the rules laid down by the world federations in hockey, football, lawn tennis, athletics, and swimming were also adopted in the East. The M.C.C. (of London) was recognized as the supreme authority in cricket, and the Hurlingham Club (London) in polo.

In 1928 a great stimulus was given to sport in pre-Partition India by the decision to take part more seriously in the World Olympic Games, especially the Olympic hockey tournament. Nearly half the players in that first hockey team were chosen from what is now Pakistan, and the team duly won the world hockey championship at the Amsterdam Games. As they were not so well trained as the Western competitors, the athletes did not prove successful. In order to enter for the Games, an Indian Olympic Association had to be formed, with branches in every province. Hockey players and athletes from the Punjab and Sind again took part in the Olympic Games of 1932 and 1936, and also helped to represent 'All-India' on other international tours and at the Western Asiatic Games.

Our great cricketers, like M. Jahangir Khan, Dilawar Hussain, Muhammed Nissar, Nazir Ali, Wazir Ali, Ameer Elahi, Baqa Jilani, Ghulam Muhammed, and Abdul Hafiz Kardar (whose names are household words in Pakistan) performed great deeds in England for the All-India Test teams of 1932, 1936, and 1946. To-day we have some splendid rising cricketers. Of an older generation we still remember with pride such grand cricketers as Shafquat, Ustad Vazir, Salamuddin, and Abdus Salam.

To hockey Pakistan has given many brilliant players such as Pinniger, Jaffir, and Ali Iqtidar Shah Dara, besides others of Olympic class. In athletics, the names of Captain S. A. Hamid, Zahur Ahmed Khan, and Lieutenant-Colonel Nazar Mohammed have brought distinction to our country. Famous Pakistani lawn tennis players are M. Sleem, Ghous Mohammed, and Iftikhar Ahmed. Gama, the champion wrestler, was world-renowned.

When the 1947 Partition took place, the entire sports system of the Indian sub-continent was immediately split into two. Pakistan and Bharat, having become completely separate countries, set up their own respective Olympic Associations and Sports Federations. One early result was that in 1948 Pakistan was able to enter its own hockey, athletics, boxing, wrestling, and swimming teams for the Olympic Games held in London, where our representatives created a very favourable impression by their sportsmanship and promising standards of performance. Our Olympic Association holds an annual athletics meeting, and has planned to send teams to important international contests in all parts of the world.

Since the 1948 Olympic Games our national football team has toured in Iran. Our Pakistan team has taken part in the World Hockey Tournament at Barcelona (in Spain) and has toured successfully in Belgium, Holland, Switzerland, and England. Our country has been represented at the Lawn Tennis Championships at Wimbledon. Our cricketers have entertained great touring sides like the West Indies XI and the Commonwealth XI, and have visited Ceylon. Pakistan is now a member of the Imperial Cricket Conference, and has thus been recognized as a great cricket country.

All these achievements have awakened high hopes in the minds of our young sportsmen. More opportunities are being created for them to take part in games and to receive proper coaching at the hands of experts. Perhaps it will not be long before we see the creation of a Pakistan Central Council of Physical Recreation, which will study the many ways in which outdoor games can best be promoted, and which will help the various sports associations with advice and also by providing training for instructors. There is a central council of that kind in Great Britain, which has paid very great attention to all outdoor games and recreations. Its members consist of all the important national sports associations. Through these the Central Council of Physical Recreation is able directly or indirectly to benefit millions of young men and women.

Both England and America have made most intelligent and attractive arrangements to keep young people interested in healthful outdoor sport. In addition to the principal games there are national associations for hiking, camping, mountain-climbing, cycling, canoeing, nature-study, open-air dancing, sailing, and riding. Working boys in Great Britain are not encouraged to spend their leisure time in idleness, but are shown how to form their own clubs, in which boxing and outdoor as well as indoor games are provided. The boys manage these clubs themselves with the help of a few grown-up people. There are similar clubs for girls. Every school has its own games masters and games mistresses. From a very early age every young British citizen is taught to look upon outdoor recreation as an ordinary part of his or her daily life. They thus grow up with a love for games and consequently become better citizens.

So also we in Pakistan, who have a natural taste for sport, can help to spread the love for games far and wide among our people. We can take part in forming more sports clubs. We can use our influence to persuade our municipalities and even our village *panchayats* to provide more sports grounds, where our young companions can spend many happy hours at football, hockey, or cricket. Not only may great players be made by such means, but the national character will be moulded on the truest and most beautiful lines.

This thought must certainly have been in the mind of the Quaid-i-Azam when he became Chief Patron of the Pakistan Olympic Association. 'Build up Pakistan higher, firmer, and stronger', he said in his special message to the organizers and competitors at the first Pakistan Olympic Games. In his speech at the opening ceremony, he added: 'I agreed to become the patron-in-chief of the Pakistan Olympic Association in the realization that the success of our people in all walks of life depends upon the cultivation of "sound minds", the natural concomitant to "sound bodies". To the athletes and youth of the nation I bid welcome. My message to you is, build up physical strength, not for aggression, not for militarism, but for becoming fighting fit, all your life and all the time in every walk of life of your nation, wherever you be, and always to be a force for peace, international amity, and goodwill. . . . Remember to win is nothing; it is the effort and the spirit behind the effort that counts.'

CHAPTER XX

WOMEN OF PAKISTAN

IN the great task of building the nation and maintaining its solidarity, women have a most valuable part to play. They are the prime architects of the character of the youth who constitute the backbone of the State. I know that in the long struggle for the achievement of Pakistan, Muslim women have stood solidly behind their men. In the bigger struggle for the building up of Pakistan that now lies ahead, let it not be said that the women of Pakistan had lagged behind or failed in their duty.—*The Quaid-i-Azam's Message to Women.*

How inspiring it is to all of us to know that the women and girls of our country have neither lagged nor failed, but that they are magnificently fulfilling the expectations of the late Quaid-i-Azam. Indeed, it is to their courage, initiative, and hard work that we owe much of the successful progress which Pakistan has made in its first few years. There is hardly a walk in life in which their good influence is not being felt.

What makes their example so noteworthy is the fact that among the cultured classes our women had long led sheltered lives. Suddenly they were called upon to face serious situations caused by the creation of Pakistan. Although many had already given up the *purdah* custom, few had previously taken an active part in public life. In the 1947 emergencies they had to make a stern choice between comfort and unfamiliar duty. They nobly chose to come forward and help their fellow-countrymen in the hour of need. Their supreme triumph came when hundreds set aside or defied age-long prejudices and offered to nurse the sick and the wounded or to look after the sorrowing bands of refugees from Bharat and Kashmir.

The seclusion of women was never sanctioned by the Holy Quran. It grew up as a custom chiefly among the wealthier or better-educated classes. In India of pre-Partition days it lingered because of its adoption in Moghal times by orthodox Hindus of the higher classes, but had begun to decline before the 1939–45 World War. There were already women in the Legislative Assemblies under the Montagu-Chelmsford Reforms (1920–37) and women took part in party politics and appeared more frequently in public. Some had become doctors and teachers. It was inevitable that seclusion should gradually be broken down. In Turkey and Iran the women had completely entered public life and the same movement had spread to other Islamic lands like Egypt. In most parts of India the Muslim peasant women had never taken to the veil because they had to work in the fields.

To-day, although the *purdah* system still prevails in some areas, it has to be acknowledged that throughout Pakistan the tendency is to abandon it. This has resulted in a great improvement in the position of women. Our Government has already decided that they will have exactly the same right to vote at elections as men. Under the Pakistan Constitution they are already full citizens of the State, free to take an equal part in all the rights, duties, and privileges of citizenship. There is nothing in the Holy Quran to forbid such a system.

Women are indeed the 'better half' of the nation. Upon them falls the greatest responsibility of all. Upon them depend the health and the safe upbringing of the children who will grow up into strong and vigorous members of the State. The management of households and the heavy burden of domestic tasks fall daily upon the women. They prepare our food, make our clothes, nurse us in our childhood illnesses, attend to the washing and mending of garments, and are busy all their waking hours. Among the peasants and poorer classes of the community large numbers work in the fields or factories, and thus help to earn extra money for the home. Even those who cannot read or write are often fountains of wisdom and experience, and they shower their loving care upon their sons and daughters, husbands and brothers.

Deep as is the debt which the country owes them in the domestic sphere, still more grateful are we to those educated women who have found time to devote their talents more directly to the well-being of Pakistan. The extent of their efforts to-day covers many occupations and professions. Most of them do not need to work. Yet they have come forward because they know that they are badly wanted. There are some occupations which cannot so well be filled by men. Even outside these lines there is wide scope for the intelligence and the point of view which a woman can bring to bear.

We find women doing great work in Pakistan as doctors, nurses, teachers, artists, makers of exquisite needlework, telephone operators, welfare workers, telegraphists, stenographers, typists, shop assistants, clerks, ambulance drivers, journalists, research scientists, radio broadcasters and auxiliaries to the Army, Navy, and Air Force—as well as spinners, weavers, carpet makers, and cottage workers in useful industries of all kinds. Among their rural occupations are cotton-picking, jute or rice planting and harvesting, silkworm-rearing, poultry-keeping, bee-keeping, herb-collecting, tea-picking, and fruit-growing. They labour in our jute and cotton factories, and at cotton-ginning. All this amounts to a tremendously big contribution through which the cultural, social, and economic life of Pakistan is enriched.

As has already been remarked, it is only in comparatively recent times that women in our country have begun to enter what may be termed the higher professions. There have always been a small proportion of well-educated women in the region now known as Pakistan. For most of the period of British rule, however, they were content to remain in the background, shedding enlightenment only in their own home circles. A few attended the girls' schools working under the old Code for European Education; others went to a few scattered colleges for women. Now at last they have come out and given Pakistan the benefit of their knowledge and experience. They are found helping as members of committees, organizers of relief and welfare work among refugees, and leaders of thought. Several have actively entered the professions for which they were trained or have offered themselves for fuller training.

These efforts are not haphazard. Our women have clear ideas about their plans to improve our nation, and they are working together as a united body and not as scattered individuals. Early in 1949 they held a conference, at which they formed the All-Pakistan Women's Association, of which Begum Liaquat Ali Khan, wife of the Prime Minister of Pakistan, was elected the first President. The Conference also chose Her Excellency Begum Nazimuddin (wife of the Governor-General of Pakistan) and Miss Fatima Jinnah (sister of the late revered Quaid-i-Azam) as Patrons. The Association, which represents the women of every province, with offices in each district, holds an annual conference, at which the lines of further progress are decided. It is a purely non-political organization, recognized by the Government and linked up with various international women's associations.

'A new nation, a new freedom, a new responsibility; these are ours to-day, and constitute a new challenge to the women of Pakistan, a challenge we cannot ignore if we are to take our proper place in the national life', said Begum Liaquat Ali Khan in her inaugural address at that historic first Conference. 'The obvious answer to this challenge is an All-Pakistan Women's Association, entirely non-political and without distinction of caste, creed, or colour, organized for the purpose of co-ordinating all efforts and policies for the cultural development, social uplift, and educational progress of the women of Pakistan. . . . Such an Association will also serve to unite us all more closely together, to obliterate the petty difference of caste, creed, and the outmoded but ever-present menace of provincialism, for it is as the citizens of Pakistan, the women of Pakistan, that we have associated ourselves together to fight the evils of ignorance, poverty, and disease, so that this land, which belongs to *all* of us and to our children, may become a happier, healthier, and better place.'

Noble words such as these have been followed up by still more noble achievements. The women have already proved their determination by their prompt and skilful handling of the tens of thousands of refugees who had suddenly poured into Lahore and Karachi from Bharat and Kashmir in the tragic years of 1947-8. It was a colossal task to provide shelter, food, clothing, medical aid, and promises of work for the hordes of widows and orphans who had escaped massacre, but who arrived destitute and hopeless after being driven from home. But there were hearts of gold to meet them. The work of rescue and of resettlement still goes on, and our All-Pakistan Women's Association will have its hands full for years with refugee-welfare and other social problems.

The need for its efforts is indeed only too clear. In Pakistan as a whole, barely six out of every hundred females can read or write; that means that roughly 37 million women and girls are completely illiterate. For the whole population of the country (80 millions), our hospitals can hardly provide more than 40,000 beds. In the Western Punjab to-day there is only one woman doctor to 150,000 of the provincial population. The shortage of nurses is also seriously great. By way of contrast, an advanced country like the United Kingdom has one doctor to every 1,000 of the population; one in every 300 persons there is a trained nurse. Every grown-up man and woman can read or write in the United Kingdom, and every child over the age of 5 goes to school. These figures show how much remains to be done in Pakistan to bring the country up to the highest levels. By coming forward to train as doctors, nurses, and teachers, our women and girls can help very considerably to make up some of the difference. These are three professions which they can take up with credit to themselves and great gain to the country as a whole.

In the sphere of practical work, Pakistani women and girls show a special talent for artistic design and the making of anything that is beautiful. They are particularly skilled in handwork; their sewing and embroidery are proverbially good. There is hardly a home where the girls do not learn these arts. Throughout the provinces we now have Women's Industrial Homes and Institutes, at which further training is given in needlework, so that regular employment is provided for women who have no other means of livelihood. These Industrial Homes have helped hundreds of refugee women to set up home again, for the Homes not only teach them how to make popular articles, but help to sell such products. They show how the beautiful old styles of embroidery and gold-thread work can be developed and adapted to modern ideas of fashion. Dress-making and modern forms of fancy needlework, both by hand and by machine, are also taught. There is a very big demand for table-cloths, cushion-covers, net embroidery, lace, crochet-work, purses, and embroidered hand-bags, which are eagerly bought for sale in Europe and America.

Nor must we forget the many useful arts and crafts which the women of Pakistan practise in their homes. Hand-spinning and weaving are traditional accomplishments. In Eastern Bengal they still make muslins of such fine texture that six yards of the material can be folded and packed into a match-box; the 'Jamdani' muslin there, with the white patterns woven into the texture, is also intensely admired. The women of Kohat, Peshawar, and Dera Ismail Khan, in the N.W.F.P., spend their leisure in making Khes bedspreads of great beauty, handsome turbans and *lungis* with richly worked end-bands of gold thread or coloured silk. In Multan and Bahawalpur they make magnificent silk turbans and waist-bands. 'Roghan' decoration on cotton is one of the most admired products of homes in Peshawar.

The list of artistic handmade wares at which Pakistani

women excel is almost endless. Particularly worthy of notice are their Multan and Baluch carpets, Hazara and Kohat *namdahs,* Waziri woollen rugs, Peshawar and Dera Ismail Khan blankets, the gorgeous *phulkari* work of West Punjab, and the exquisite embroidery with small pieces of glass worked into the design which is a speciality of Sind. These and other articles, such as lamp-shades, wicker baskets, fans, shopping-bags, and paper pottery, are much sought after in Great Britain and the United States, who are big customers for Pakistan's home products. Through the Pakistan Cottage Industries Association many such items were sent as exhibits to the Women's International Exposition at New York, where they proved extremely popular among Western purchasers.

Through all these various methods the women of our country are steadily helping to improve their own lot in life. A great deal remains to be done. Wonderful progress, however, has already been made, and many wholesome influences are at work. Great possibilities, for instance, arise out of such movements as the All-Pakistan Girl Guides' Association, whose membership is now close upon 10,000. The Girl Guides played a worthy part in helping the refugees, especially refugee children, to whom they brought much cheer and comfort by organizing games and by teaching reading, writing, knitting, and simple handicrafts. Pakistan Girl Guides have been able to represent their country at world Guide gatherings in Great Britain and Europe.

Most promising, too, is the creation of the Pakistan Women's National Guard, which is a recognized part of our country's defence. Although meant chiefly to assist the Pakistan Medical Service, it is a disciplined body of volunteers well trained in self-defence and the handling of arms. Its members undergo regular courses in drill, physical training, Red Cross work, nursing, First-Aid and Air Raid Precautions. A similar corps, called the Pakistan Women's Naval Reserve, is attached to the Pakistan Navy. In times of national emergency both these organizations will prove most valuable, especially in relieving men of some of the non-combatant duties.

Three years is a very brief page in the history of a nation. Already, however, in so short a time the women of Pakistan have succeeded in proving that there is no aspect of our life in which they are not able to perform their due share of work. Their achievements command respect and admiration. They are true patriots. They point the road and keep step in our march to progress.

CHAPTER XXI

IN THE SERVICE OF THE PUBLIC

WE have been reading about the very large number of activities which have to be carried on daily for the well-being and contentment of the public. The defence of our country, health, education, agriculture, irrigation, industrial progress, transport, postal and telegraphic services and co-operative societies have been the subjects of some of the previous chapters of this book. We have had many references to the part that the Government plays in promoting all these phases of our daily existence.

The Government, as we have already learnt, is the machinery through which our nation manages all its affairs. It includes our Federal and Provincial Legislative Assemblies, our Ministers, and the Departments which they control. They receive their orders from 'the people' at the time of general elections and are constantly in touch with the opinions of the people. As we have seen, we are a democracy—a State in which the Government *of* the people is carried on *by* the people and *for* the people.

The will of the people is the sovereign power in Pakistan; there is no human power superior to their will, and they exercise that will through the Legislatures and the Ministers, whom they authorize to act in their name. Even when no elections are taking place, the will of the people is made known at all times through various means. There are the newspapers, which report all that is happening, and which publish the speeches or letters of public spokesmen. Meetings of political parties and associations are held all the year round and give the people an opportunity to voice their opinions. There are frequent public functions at which addresses are given by prominent persons and discussions held. Our merchants and industrialists also have their Chambers of Commerce and other associations, by means of which they can tell the Government and the public about business developments and the way that things should be done.

It is because 'freedom of speech' and 'freedom of association' are part of their daily existence, clearly proclaimed in the Pakistan constitution, that our people can claim to be a real sovereign power. One has only to glance through the pages of a newspaper to realize the existence of the freedom of speech (and of writing), for columns are devoted to the reporting of debates and speeches, to 'Letters to the Editor', and to editorial comment. The will of the people is thus made known every day and about anything that concerns the country. The people have the right freely to speak about their grievances and complaints, their praise and suggestions, aims and ideals, and to state their arguments; the right also to meet together—so long as their actions are for a lawful purpose and not injurious to the best interests of the country. The sum total of all these utterances is known as 'public opinion'.

The will of the people is, as we have seen, exercised through the Legislative Assemblies. These, however, are not in constant session; their meetings do not take place every day, but only during some periods of the year. They accordingly have to entrust their power and authority into the hands of the Ministers. Since the

Ministers have a great deal of work to do, they need the help of various trained officials who are given certain duties to perform, and who are paid for their services according to their ability and their responsibilities.

In a large modern civilized country so many things have to be done in a regular manner and for so wide an area that a great mass of details requires daily attention. The work has to be divided in such a way that the most difficult problems and the general direction and supervision are handed over to the cleverest and most experienced officials. To help and advise them are specialist officers and executive officers, and under these are a large number of clerical officers and assistants. In addition there are messengers, workmen, and outdoor staff, employed by the Government. All are paid salaries or wages. They form the great body of public servants known as the Civil Service, who of course do not include the Armed Forces.

Since the welfare of many millions of people is at stake, the Government has to be businesslike in its methods. Its Ministers and their higher officers have therefore to arrange sound business systems so that the decisions they make are always correct and mistakes are rare. They also have to control the staffs, totalling in some cases thousands of people in one department alone—as in the case of the railways or the postal and telegraph service. For general guidance a great number of rules and regulations have to be prepared and observed, so that each individual should be treated justly and know his own duties exactly. Careful records have to be kept, in order that every action of the Government can be referred to again. Accurate accounts of income and expenditure have also to be maintained, because all the money belongs really to the country as a whole. At any time the Government's actions can be made the subject of questions in the Assemblies, and these must be answered because the Departments are responsible to the Assemblies and, through them, therefore, to the sovereign will of the people.

The actual administration of a country is thus by no means a simple task. It calls for much planning and organization. Success naturally depends largely on the quality of the Civil Service as a whole. The first requisite is that Civil Servants of all grades should be suitably educated and trained. Their work makes it necessary that they should be able, not only to read and write, but understand a great many things. Even the humblest messengers should at least be literate. The higher officials and specialists should be men of real intellect, able to grasp the most difficult of problems and to take the initiative in preparing schemes.

Equally important is the need to make sure that every servant of the Government, high or lowly, is a 'good man'. All must be completely honest and trustworthy people, impartial and incorruptible. The one thing above all else that the public want from their civil servants is absolute fairness in their dealings. The messenger who demands 'baksheesh', the clerk who expects a bribe, or a higher officer who would do a favour in exchange for a gift, are not only law-breakers, but a cause of discontent among the people. The honest civil servant, on the other hand, knows that he is already being paid proper wages by the public for duly attending to their needs, and that he would be bringing shame upon himself and his office by giving in to the temptation of accepting a further reward. Even more criminal is the action of those members of the general public who try to bribe a civil servant or

IN THE SERVICE OF THE PUBLIC

offer him any kind of illegal gratification. When detected they are severely punished and well deserve their disgrace. Bribery is a very serious social offence, for it causes injustice to honest persons who refrain from this form of law-breaking, and it also undermines public confidence in the administration.

From the very start the Pakistan Government decided to make sure that the highest possible standard of conduct should prevail in our public services. In his first speech to the Constituent Assembly of Pakistan the Quaid-i-Azam said: 'One of the biggest curses from which India is suffering—I do not say that other countries are free from it, but I think our condition is much worse—is bribery and corruption. That really is a poison. We must put that down with an iron hand, and I hope that you will take adequate measures as soon as it is possible for this Assembly to do so.' Since then a law has been passed to ensure speedier trials and effective punishment of corrupt offenders. The position has greatly improved, and we can now say that few Government servants give way to temptation.

The selection of all officers and clerks of the country's civil service is carried out with special care. Every candidate has to produce reliable evidence of his moral suitability. Educational standards are tested by means of competitive examinations. For the higher grades the minimum qualification is a good Honours Degree. The examinations are conducted by the Pakistan Public Services Commission, which makes the final appointments after having interviewed the applicants.

It is a distinction to be chosen for the Civil Service, for the successful candidate knows that he will be given splendid opportunities to promote the well-being of his fellow-countrymen. To the real patriot this means even more than the gaining of a secure post with many privileges and a good pension on which eventually to retire. There are no barriers to promotion for those who are suitably qualified and who improve their own knowledge and experience. The capable clerk can rise to the executive and higher grades and make use of his talents for the good of his country. Those who specialize can be raised to positions of great responsibility and usefulness. By its training schemes the Government is able to encourage its more ambitious servants to ascend to the highest rungs of the administrative ladder.

The selection of the best available persons for certain special appointments, particularly those requiring technical qualifications, is essential in a progressive country. It cannot be done satisfactorily through competitive examinations, because mere book learning does not prove complete suitability; a candidate has also to possess the right personality and experience—otherwise there is the danger of placing 'a square peg in a round hole'. As soon as a Ministry informs the Pakistan Public Service Commission that a special appointment is about to be made in any Department, the Recruitment Branch of the Commission sends an advertisement to all the leading English and Urdu newspapers in Pakistan as well as in Bharat (and sometimes even in Great Britain and the United States) and an announcement is made over Radio Pakistan. Copies of the advertisement are also displayed at all Employment Exchanges in Pakistan.

In this way wide publicity is given to a vacancy and suitable candidates are able to submit their applications. Those that have the best qualifications are then called to attend interviews with the Commission at central places like Karachi, Lahore, Dacca, Rawalpindi, Peshawar, and Chittagong. There they are asked, not only about the examinations which they have passed or the work they have already done, but sometimes also about social and general topics. These questions aim purely at testing the candidate's level of intelligence, the extent of his general knowledge, and his strength of character. This system makes certain that there can be no favouritism or 'jobbery' and that no candidate is selected merely because he happens to be related to some important person. There is no 'back door' to the public services. Only the really deserving candidate can hope to enter, and the people can thus feel confident that the best man is chosen for a Government appointment.

The Departments into which the work of the Government is divided are named and planned according to the nature of their respective activities. Both Federal and Provincial Governments have their Departments which are in the charge of their own Ministers. Sometimes a Minister looks after several Departments. The principal Departments are named on the next page.

From this list it might appear that there is a certain amount of overlapping between the Central (Federal) and Provincial Governments. This, however, is not completely the case. We have to remember that each has its own sphere: the Federal Government deals with questions which concern the country as a whole, and a Provincial Government takes up matters which concern its own territory. In somewhat the same way the Headmaster or Principal of a school looks after the school as a whole, while each of the masters is expected to deal primarily with his own classroom—though, of course, they consult each other often. There is always close

PRINCIPAL DEPARTMENTS OF GOVERNMENT

Federal (Concerning the country as a whole)	*Provincial* (Concerning only the provinces)
1. Foreign Relations and Commonwealth Relations.	1. Education.
2. Defence.	2. Health and Medical.
3. Transport and Communications.	3. Local Self-government.
4. Finance.	4. Industry and Technical Education.
5. Health.	5. Agriculture.
6. Education.	6. Public Works.
7. Irrigation.	7. Co-operation.
8. Industrial Development.	8. Labour.
9. Trade and Commerce.	9. Roads.
10. Interior, Information, Broadcasting.	10. Land Tenancy.
11. Public Works (Central).	11. Animal Husbandry.
12. Law.	12. Police.
13. Labour.	13. Medical.
14. Customs and Excise.	14. Information.
15. Archæology.	15. Jails and Reformatories.
16. Weather Study.	16. Forestry.

contact between the Federal and Provincial Governments, and the Centre is usually able to give each of the provinces a good deal of help and advice.

While the actual day-to-day carrying on of the Departments' business is done by their officials and assistants, our Government makes much use of the Committee system. This is a common practice in all democratic countries. The Committees do not consist only of officials, but contain many non-officials. The Government is thus able to obtain a great deal of information and advice from businessmen and experts who have valuable suggestions to offer. By this means the Ministers and Departments are kept in close touch with public opinion and much other useful knowledge, and are able to deal with important questions and plans from the broadest points of view. As a rule the non-official members of the committees are not paid any salaries by the Government, but are entitled to repayments of their travel and other ordinary expenses when attending the committee meetings.

Both the Central (Federal) and Provincial Governments have many such committees. The most important of all is the 'Planning Advisory Board', consisting of officials and leading industrialists, bankers, businessmen, and merchants, which helps the Development Board of the Pakistan Government in the preparation of great new schemes to improve the country's welfare as well as to re-examine old schemes. These Boards have already helped our country to start huge new enterprises in irrigation, utilization of power resources, forestry, agriculture, the search for mineral wealth, the construction of new ports and other beneficial developments.

The system of combining both officials and non-officials in such Committees and Boards is doubly valuable, because it enables every well-informed person and numerous business associations to feel that they are taking a big and worthy share in the shaping of Pakistan's destinies. They are thus not cut off from the official and administrative sides, and are glad to use their influence among their own experts and workers to promote beneficial projects. Being in the position of trustees of the public will, the Government welcomes such a useful method of learning what is in the best interests of the people. Such co-operation, freely given by both sides, is one of the brightest omens of Pakistan's future progress.

CHAPTER XXII

OUR CULTURAL HERITAGE

Not being merely an animal, but gifted with an inventive mind and an emotional nature, Man has from very early times tried to make his life as agreeable as possible. Even when forced to exist in surroundings of great hardship, he has always looked for opportunities to rise above his circumstances. The earliest traces of human abodes have usually preserved at least some slight evidence of man's search for the things that pleased him. He was not content to possess the five senses of sight, hearing, taste, touch, and smell, but learned by experience and reason how to stimulate these by his own efforts.

In the caves which sheltered them thousands of years ago, we still discover relics to show how primitive men and women deliberately made or collected such things as could bring a little pleasure into their hard lives. They wore simple, brightly coloured ornaments made of shell or bone. They drew pictures on the walls and on the rocks of their dwellings. They adorned their own naked bodies with paint and with feathers, or with the skins of the wild beasts they had slain. There are still savage tribes in some parts of the world where such customs exist. Man also liked to hear pleasant sounds, and found that he could sing; his love for music led him to make simple instruments such as conches, drums, rough flutes, and single-stringed harps, from which he could produce pleasing notes and exciting rhythm.

OUR CULTURAL HERITAGE

As man gradually became more civilized, his conscious efforts to subdue his surroundings to his better comfort and liking developed in him some special tastes. He began to pick and choose those activities or articles which gave him more pleasure, and to study the arts which interested his mind. It was only natural, also, that he should be influenced by his surroundings, and that in consequence the forest dweller should find his imagination stirred by the mysterious happenings of the gloomy woodlands. The ocean would leave something different in the way of impressions on the minds of those who lived by the seashore. The mountain people would gain a still different idea of life. Thus, although their aim was the common one of striving for better ease and mental pleasure, their means of expressing their emotions would take widely different forms.

In this way, perhaps, there developed many different kinds of human culture. The word 'culture' simply means what we have just been reading about—the deliberate effort to rise superior to our primitive surroundings by making and using the things that bring comfort and pleasure of both body and mind. As human beings learnt to communicate with each other by spoken and written words and by trade and travel, the entire range of their cultural interests became widened. They could learn from each other many new arts and discover many new objects. Their earliest impressions and constant surroundings, however, would naturally continue to exert the strongest influence on their minds.

Culture has always played a prominent part in the history of nations. As civilization spread and became more complicated, the natural preferences found more means of expression and tastes became more specialized. Man's ear for rhythm and for music was no longer satisfied by single monotonous sounds, but discovered that greater pleasure was to be gained from 'harmony' (the mingling of notes in agreement) and from 'orchestration' (the playing of several different kinds of instruments together). Music thus gained a new meaning. So also it gave men more delight to add various colours to a rough line drawing—and thus the art of painting was discovered. Ordinary speech became more melodious by the introduction of metre and rhyme; hence the invention of poetry. From mere recitation or dumb posing, there arose the arts of drama and play acting.

For the four or five thousand years during which human beings have been growing civilized, there has been going on this process of refinement of tastes and modes of expression. When we speak of the culture of a nation, therefore, we mean the degree to which it has perfected the finer arts and risen above the level of the savage. Culture denotes, in fact, the ability to bring grace and elegance and beauty into the people's way of living. It may and does differ in the case of various nations, according to the surroundings in which they exist or according to their history and their associations with other races. There are still some nations which have not risen to a high level of culture, whereas others have rich traditions of beauty and art. Among these better-favoured nations Pakistan holds a high place.

Pakistan owes its culture to the oft-repeated contact between East and West which forms its 5,000 years of known history. Being situated at the gateways of the Indian sub-continent, over its western plains swept repeated hosts of invaders who already possessed high standards of civilization. Owing to the dense mountain forests on our far-eastern boundary, the influences which happened to penetrate from China and Burma into Assam and Eastern Bengal were much slighter and left almost no permanent impression. The early Aryan invaders from our north-west frontier drove the primitive aboriginal tribes into the central parts of India and were themselves followed and overcome by Greeks, Arabs, Turkomans, Afghans, Moghals, and Iranians. Even Eastern Pakistan felt the effects of these great upheavals, and Islamic influences had spread widely there long before the Moghals occupied that region. Owing to the presence of dense forests and wide rivers, however, Eastern Pakistan developed in isolation, whereas Western Pakistan was for centuries a melting-pot of many different races.

The outstanding fact, nevertheless, is that between the conquest of Sind by Mohammed Bin Qasim in A.D. 711 and the decline of the Moghal Empire after Ahmad Shah Durani's invasions during the eighteenth century, Western Pakistan was for roughly over a thousand years completely under Islamic influence and government. Hinduism had lingered, because of Islamic tolerance, and the brief period of Sikh ascendancy had not yet arrived. Nearly all the contacts of the local inhabitants were Islamic, and the different invaders brought with them a more or less uniform culture—the Culture of Islam. At an early stage many Hindus, in both Western and Eastern Pakistan, voluntarily accepted Islam, because they were impressed by its tolerance and spirit of universal brotherhood.

Added to this was the fact that the whole of Islam, which at one time had spread far into Europe and all along the North African coast, had adopted the Arabic language and civilization. This gave an early unity of spirit to all the various Muslim nations. Even the later Persians had been stimulated by Arabic influences; so also were the Turkis. These three were easily fused into one people in Northern India, whom to-day we call Pakistanis. Whether their ancestors came from Arabia, Mesopotamia, Turkestan, Iran, or Mongolia, the resulting population were brought up on and absorbed the common culture and civilization, which was essentially of Arabic origin.

Being completely distinct from the Hindus in the most fundamental of their religious beliefs, the Muslims remained as a people apart, all over India. The culture of the Muslims came to them from its Arabic source. Hinduism was a creed and a system of so completely different a nature that there could be no common meeting-ground. Hence, for over a thousand years the two lived side by side in the same country, but as two separate nations with two separate cultural systems. Only in a social sense could they mingle at the edges—one manifestation of which was the gradual making of a new spoken language, Hindustani. Even here, however, they met only to part again, over the written form which their speech should take.

As was natural, during the thousand years of Muslim ascendancy in India, the languages brought by the Islamic conquerors became the widest in use, especially for court and official purposes. Being somewhat allied, the three (Persian, Turki, and Arabic) easily became one tongue, which also absorbed many words from the dialects of Hindustan. It quickly grew into a rich and melodious new language known as Hindvi, Hindi, and later as Urdu. By the year A.D. 1300 it had its first great poet (Amir Khusro, of Delhi), and many others followed. Amir Khusro, who was a famous historian, courtier, scholar, and musician, also introduced new systems of dancing and of music, blending the Persian and Indian styles, with the Turki and Persian influence uppermost. There remains a striking similarity between Pakistani dancing and music and the same arts as practised in Eastern Turkestan to-day. This Turki and Persian influence can be seen in several other directions, especially in the costumes and manners of Pakistan women and in the social atmosphere as well as on many ceremonial occasions.

The wonderful ease with which the Islamic spirit is able to absorb and adapt agreeable features from other cultural systems is revealed most impressively in the architectural glories of Pakistan. Some of the most beautiful examples have been left on the Bharat side—notably the Taj Mahal (Agra), the Jama Masjid and Shah Jehan's fort (Delhi), and the splendid buildings of Akbar's deserted capital, Fatehpur Sikri. Even so, however, we have in Pakistan the imposing Lahore Fort, to whose magnificence Akbar, Jahangir, Shahjahan, and Aurangzeb in turn made their contributions; the tombs of Mariam Zameni, Anarkali, and Jahangir in or near Lahore; the stately Shalimar Garden; the dignified Badshahi Mosque to the west of Lahore Fort; and many other great examples of Moghal architecture. In Eastern Pakistan also we find numerous interesting structures of classical design, dating from early Moghal times. Here again is revealed the inherent unity which prevails in the cultural traditions of our country.

Painting was another art in which the Moghals excelled, and in which Islamic influence still predominates.

The beauty of Kashmiri carving, lacquer work, papier-mâché, and woollen and silk creations is world-renowned. There is scarcely anything else anywhere to compare with the glorious gold and silver filigree work of East Bengal and Western Pakistan, while the carpets of Baluchistan, Kashmir, and the N.W.F.P. have preserved the highest traditions that made the craftsmen of Persia and Bokhara fabled in olden days. In all these arts, and others like pottery, embroidery, and art needlework, the influence of Islamic culture is ever present.

From the poetry of handicrafts to the poetry of words is but a change in the medium of expression and not in the spirit of our culture. Of all our finer arts, Urdu poetry has remained perhaps the most loyal to the original purity of Islamic culture. From Amir Khusro until our present age we have had a continuous stream of classical verse flowing from a hundred pens. Vali of the Deccan, Sultan Quil Qutub Shah, Sanda, Mir Taqi Mir, Asadullah Khan Ghalib, Momin Khan Momin, Mohammed Iqbal—these are more than names to every schoolchild and grown-up person. So also are other great literary figures, such as Shah Abdul Latif, of Bhit, Khusal Khan Khatak, Abdul Rahman, Kazim Khan Shaida, and Ali Khan, whose works are widely read.

Although Pakistan has been so fortunate as to preserve its cultural traditions in much of their purity, it is a sign of strength that a narrowness of outlook has been avoided. In our own day we have many close contacts with the culture of other Islamic lands. One of the earliest events after the founding of Pakistan was the creation of a Cultural Relations Committee with the express purpose of fostering friendly relations with other countries of the world. A Pakistan-Turkish Cultural Association has been formed, and this has already enabled many eager students to begin learning the Turkish language and listening to Turkish poetry recitations. Our Pakistan-Arab Cultural Association is actively promoting the study of the Holy Quran, the Arabic language, and the Arabic (*naskh*) script, and has established a most useful Arabic College. At the inauguration of the Pakistan-Iran Cultural Association, a musical rendering of 'In a Persian Garden' and tableaux from Omar Khayyám were delightful new experiences.

All over Pakistan to-day—from Sind to Eastern Bengal—lively interest is being shown in the cultivation of literature in all the languages of our country. Many young new writers have come to the front. There is a remarkable development especially in Bengali literature, which is breaking free from heavy Sanskrit words and adopting far more Urdu, Persian, and Arabic words. The movement to write Bengali in Arabic script has also been revived, so as to bring Bengali into line with the language of other Islamic countries. The mind of the whole nation is awake and glorying to-day in its cultural attainments, while the world watches in approval. It is a sign of spiritual grace and strength of character when a nation can take pride in its cultural traditions as well as in its material progress.

CHAPTER XXIII

PAKISTAN'S PLACE IN THE BRITISH COMMONWEALTH

ALL people like to know that they have some particularly good friends on whom they can rely, and whom they can in their own turn help in good or troubled times alike. The friends they value most are not the chance acquaintances they make in the ordinary course of business, but those friends who are bound to them by old-established ties of mutual help, admiration, and loyalty. Between such there exists a feeling of equal partnership and strong common interest; what harms one is hurtful to all the others of the same group, and what is beneficial to one brings equal satisfaction to his fellows.

This is true also of countries, especially those countries which at some time in history have been held more closely together than by mere alliances. The 'British Commonwealth of Nations' is an outstanding example. In its present form it is somewhat different from the 'British Empire' which existed until very recently. It remains nevertheless a closely related association of countries, most of whom still regard the King of England as their own King, although in reality they are completely free to govern themselves exactly as they wish and even to give up membership of the Commonwealth.

The Commonwealth to-day consists of the following countries: (1) The United Kingdom of England, Scotland, Wales, and Northern Ireland, and the dependent

PLACE IN THE BRITISH COMMONWEALTH

colonies; (2) the fully self-governing members of the Commonwealth—(*a*) Canada, (*b*) Australia, (*c*) New Zealand, (*d*) South Africa, (*e*) Pakistan, (*f*) Ceylon, and (*g*) Southern Rhodesia; and (3) the associated Republics of (*a*) Ireland and (*b*) Bharat. It will be noticed that Burma is no longer in the list; that country became separated from British India in 1935 and left the Commonwealth in 1946—it is now a completely separate land.

Strictly speaking, the British Empire lasted for only seventy years—from 1877, when Queen Victoria was first proclaimed Empress of India, until 1947, when 'India' was divided into Pakistan and Bharat. The King himself gave up the title of 'Emperor' in 1947 by Act of Parliament. He remains the symbol of unity only in the United Kingdom, the Colonies, and the Self-governing Dominions.

Historically, however, the British Empire was a great influence in the world. It brought 550 million people (one-fifth of the whole human race) under one ruler and one flag. Its origin dates back to the reign of Queen Elizabeth, when England's naval victories over Spain and Portugal made her mistress of the seas and enabled her to establish small settlements on the east coast of North America. In 1600 was formed the East India Company, which later became so strong that it carried on war successfully with the French and Moghals in India. This great English trading concern in fact became the ruler of so large a portion of the country that it could not carry out the work of government sufficiently well. In 1858, therefore, after the Mutiny, all the powers of the Company were transferred to the Crown, which, as we have already noted, took over the Imperial title that the Moghal rulers had previously held.

Meanwhile, the search for trade had led the English into many other far-distant parts of the world and also into several wars, which ended in victories for the British forces and one by one added new colonies. There was one serious defeat—when some of the North American colonies broke away and formed an independent country under the name of 'The United States of America'. Canada, however, remained loyal to Britain. Later, Australia and New Zealand were discovered, and British settlers went to those new lands as well as to South Africa. The Boer War of 1899–1902 led to the conquest of several provinces in South Africa, and in 1910 these were formed into the Dominion known as the Union of South Africa. Australia, New Zealand, and Canada were also converted into self-governing Dominions.

Trade and warfare had also added several other parts of the world to Britain's possessions overseas. Gibraltar, Malta, Cyprus, Aden, Bahrein, Port Sudan, and Hong Kong were occupied and held as important outposts guarding Britain's sea routes to the East. The West Indies, portions of the north coast of South America, Ceylon, Burma, the Straits Settlements, Somaliland, British North Borneo, and several large tracts along the coast of West Africa (Nigeria, the Gold Coast, Sierra Leone, and Gambia), and numerous large or small islands scattered all over the oceans—one by one, at different dates, all these came under the British flag and were developed as colonies. The desire to end slavery led the British also into Zanzibar, on the east coast of Africa, Uganda and Kenya, while English traders and settlers colonized the Rhodesias. Southern Rhodesia has now the status of a self-governing Dominion. During World War I (1914–18) the British drove the Germans out of

Tanganyika, and took charge of this territory as a Mandate under the League of Nations.

With the exception of the Indian sub-continent, Burma, Ceylon, and Southern Rhodesia, Britain's tropical possessions and dependencies have remained as colonies and do not yet govern themselves. They are under the control of the British Parliament, acting through the Colonial Secretary to His Majesty's Government in London. Their people have only recently begun to shed their ignorance and backward condition. As they become better educated and more able to manage their own affairs, they can be raised to the position of self-governing Dominions. That is the aim of the British, who are encouraging the West Indians, West Africans, East Africans, Malayans, Sudanese, and other subject races to train and prepare for that goal.

Of more direct interest to Pakistan are our fellow-members of the Commonwealth which, like ourselves, have already become independent self-governing units of the British Commonwealth. Although we are a newly formed country, we have much in common with Canada, Australia, New Zealand, Ceylon, and South Africa, as well as with the United Kingdom itself. All members of the Commonwealth are equally free, equal in status, in no way subordinate one to another in any aspect of our domestic or external affairs, though recognizing the Crown as a symbol of unity. We stand together because we want to.

Strangely enough, there are no artificial ties. There is no central 'Commonwealth Legislature', no central judiciary or defence system, and no uniform foreign policy. Yet the Dominions manage to work together as if according to an agreed plan. This is done by frequent consultation and discussion amongst themselves, for which there exist suitable methods.

Commonwealth Consultations

It is important to remember that the affairs of the Dominions—that is, the self-governing members of the Commonwealth, as distinct from the Colonial territories—are not 'run' from London. Each of the Dominions is fully independent, and the United Kingdom has the same status as any other Dominion. Relations between the Dominions are conducted through a process of consultation. Each Dominion has its High Commissioner (or, if it is a Republic, its Ambassador) in the capital of each other Dominion. The High Commissioners and Ambassadors are the main channel of communication between Governments. Through them, each Dominion Government is kept informed of the activities and policies of the Governments of the other Dominions and, on occasions, all meet together to discuss problems which affect the Commonwealth as a whole.

From time to time it becomes necessary for 'family councils' to be held, whenever events in other parts of the world, or within the Commonwealth itself, call for specially important decisions. These 'family councils' take the form of meetings of Ministers, which may be held in any of the Commonwealth capitals; for instance, only so recently as 1950 the Foreign Ministers of the Dominions all met in Colombo to discuss questions of policy affecting the Commonwealth as a whole. Or there may be meetings of Prime Ministers—there have been several since 1916—or meetings of Finance Ministers to talk over between themselves problems in their own special fields.

The United Kingdom Government's relations with the other members of the Commonwealth are conducted through an office in London called the Commonwealth Relations Office. This is the machine through which the United Kingdom Government and Parliament are kept fully informed of all that is happening in the Commonwealth, and, in the other direction, the means of keeping the Governments of the Dominions fully and quickly informed about happenings and opinions in the United Kingdom. Through this office there passes a ceaseless flow of telegrams and reports to and from the United Kingdom representatives in the other capitals of the Commonwealth—Delhi, Karachi, Colombo, Ottawa, Canberra, Wellington, and Capetown. Consultation—the exchanging of views on all matters concerning two or more of the Dominions or the Commonwealth as a whole; a sharing of secrets, possible only among a 'family' of nations—that is the way in which the Commonwealth works.

A second means of working together is through various Commonwealth consultative bodies, which attend to technical matters. Examples are the Imperial Economic Committee, the Imperial Shipping Committee, the Executive Council of the Imperial Agricultural Bureau, and the Committee of Imperial Defence. In addition there are numerous other official and private associations working on a co-operative Commonwealth basis. Taken together, they form a vital part of the structure of the British Commonwealth.

Pakistan derives many common benefits and advantages by its membership of the Commonwealth. It

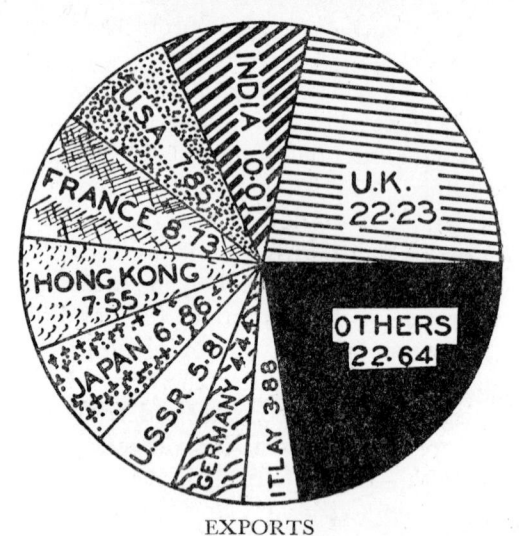

EXPORTS
Direction of Sea-borne Trade, 1949–50

shares in the trade 'preferences' given to each other by the members of the Commonwealth, so that smaller customs duties are charged on our products in the Commonwealth markets. Pakistanis are able to travel freely and safely throughout the Commonwealth. They are able to take part in each other's Defence Training schemes and social services. Some of the capital which we need for the development of our country is readily available through our Commonwealth connection without any loss to our sense of independence.

This close linking up is helped also by the exchange of High Commissioners, who act as a kind of Ambassador. Pakistan has its own High Commissioners in the United Kingdom, Australia, New Zealand, Canada, South Africa, Ceylon and Bharat, and there is always a High

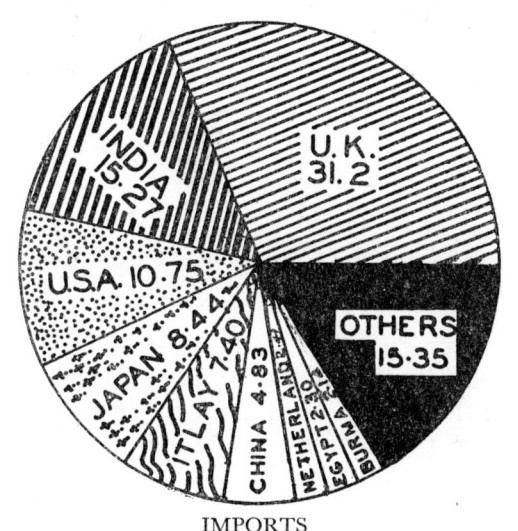

IMPORTS
Direction of Sea-borne Trade, 1949–50

Commissioner from each of these countries present in Karachi. At all the Dominion capitals these representatives are in daily touch with each other, and can thus act together quickly on matters of any kind.

Pakistan to-day is of greater importance to the British Commonwealth of Nations than most people realize. Although not the largest Dominion in point of area, it is easily first so far as population is concerned. This does not, of course, include the 'associate' Republic of Bharat. The table on the next page will help us roughly to compare the various Commonwealth countries.

Quite apart from mere numbers, the population of Pakistan includes a large proportion of men with great martial traditions, who formed the flower of the 'Indian Army' of pre-Partition days, and who served the Empire

	Area in square miles	Total population
Canada	3,694,800	11,419,000
Australia	2,977,600	7,000,000
South Africa	472,550	10,341,000
New Zealand	104,850	1,628,900
United Kingdom	94,200	47,000,000
Pakistan	360,780	82,000,000
Eire	26,959	2,968,000
Bharat	1,440,000	330,000,000

with outstanding valour in two World Wars. Pakistanis shed their blood with that of Britons, Canadians, Australians, New Zealanders, and South Africans on many a battlefield. A people of keen intelligence, they are fighting material of the highest quality. In a crisis they can count on their past services not being forgotten by their former comrades, who are still their Commonwealth colleagues.

As guardian of a frontier not far removed from the zones of Russian influence in the north-west and Chinese turmoil in the east, Pakistan occupies a strategic position, the significance of which is only now beginning to be understood. The Commonwealth countries can therefore be expected to watch with more than ordinary interest the efforts of a democratic nation like ours to develop our resources, and increase our efficiency and make our strength secure. There is a growing realization amongst them that Pakistan counts for much within the Commonwealth. This is a feeling shared, too, by all democratic nations, for, as we shall read in our next chapters, Pakistan has a role to fill in the daily affairs of the world as a whole. Loving freedom and peace, we can by our efforts and our influence in the United Nations Organization help to preserve the peace of the world.

CHAPTER XXIV

OUR NEAREST NEIGHBOURS

ALTHOUGH only four large independent countries have a long common frontier with Eastern and Western Pakistan, at least two other great and powerful nations are close enough to deserve attention. A seventh adjoining territory, Kashmir, has from the start been a grave problem, because both Pakistan and Bharat claim it as their own, and up to the moment of writing this book the fate of Kashmir has not been decided. We need to know something more about all these lands.

Our largest common frontier is with Bharat, which almost completely surrounds Eastern Pakistan, and which forms the whole of the eastern boundary of Western Pakistan. The Rajputana States of Jodhpur and Bikaner might have formed a buffer territory here, but they were absorbed into Bharat and have practically ceased to exist; they have no independence of their own and are in fact now part of Bharat.

A tour of our borders might conveniently start from a midway point on the northern shores of the Arabian Sea, close to the mouth of the Dasht River. To the east is the district of Makran; to the west lies Persia. The boundary continues in a northerly direction for about 550 miles, separating Baluchistan from Persia. At Koh-i-Malik Shah, our boundary line suddenly runs from west to east, separating Baluchistan from the southern barren portion of Afghanistan known as the Helmand Desert. Persia is left far behind and our neighbour now becomes Afghanistan.

From near Nushki the Afghan-Pakistan frontier again zigzags northwards for over 1,000 miles, to the apex of the Gilgit area at the Beyik Pass high in the Pamir mountain ranges. The real barrier dividing Afghanistan and Pakistan consists of a series of lofty and rugged mountain chains running north and south, parallel to each other, and pierced only by a few difficult passes. It was through such passes as these, chiefly the Bolan Pass (near Quetta) and the Khyber Pass (near Peshawar), that Greek and Islamic invaders poured into India.

From the Gilgit apex our border line turns sharply south and then curves eastwards, leaving Kashmir beyond it. Where Sialkot and Gurdaspore districts meet, the line for the first time divides Pakistan from Bharat. The boundary now takes a southerly direction for several hundred miles and turns at right angles westwards till the Rann of Kutch is reached.

Turning for a few minutes to the map of Eastern Pakistan, we notice how that province is bordered by West Bengal on the west, Assam on the north, and Assam and Tripura State on most of the eastern side. All these areas are Bharati territory. Only at its lower portion does the eastern frontier march alongside Burma, separating the latter from Pakistan's Chittagong Hill Tracts and from the extreme lower tip of Chittagong District.

At no point does Soviet Russia come into direct touch with Pakistan. The Chinese westernmost province of Sunkiang lies alongside the West Pakistan north-eastern frontier for only a short distance. Yet these two cannot be ignored when we study our own country's position, for they are extremely close, if not actually next-door, neighbours. In the far north, an observer standing on the high mountains can in fact look down on five different lands—Afghanistan to the west, Russia in the north, Chinese Turkestan to the east, Kashmir in the south-east, and Pakistan (Tribal territory) in the south-west—all within a few miles of each other.

Returning to our starting-points of Mekran and Baluchistan, we can rejoice to find that our neighbour there is the friendly and fellow-Islamic land of Persia. For a few years Persia preferred to be known as Iran, but has now readopted its ancient name, famous in history for over 2,500 years. Long before Western Europe gained its first glimpses of civilized life, Persia was already a great centre of world culture. Through it passed the six principal trade routes of Asia, where caravans from many lands crossed each other. The early civilizations of Media, Assyria, Asia Minor, Greece, and Egypt penetrated deep into Persia, which was well known also to Rome and the ancient rulers of India. Later the Arabs conquered the land. Mongol invaders followed, ruthlessly destroying its cities and its trade.

From all these disasters the Persians not only survived, but recovered their strength. Their power of absorbing the best characteristics and culture of their conquerors was so amazing that they in turn were able to set out under Nadir Shah to defeat the declining Moghal power in India. Again and again Persia recovered, and more than once enjoyed a 'Golden Age' of prosperity. In all the arts of peace her people excelled. Ferdousi, their greatest epic poet, had many notable companions such as Faruki of Sistan, the 'poet of joy', Abu Raihan Beruni, the scientist, and Abu Sina, the physician, with Omar Khayyám as perhaps the symbol of them all in that post-Islamic era.

Persia was not only the melting-pot of many cultural systems, but the reservoir whence culture flowed to other lands, including Pakistan. There is a striking similarity between the two countries, which to-day seem to share the same spirit of progress in addition to the same Islamic love of freedom, equality, justice, and toleration. We are happy to remember that the historic ties of friendship between us were lately strengthened by the visit paid by His Imperial Majesty the Shahenshah Mohammed Reza Phlavi to Pakistan in the spring of 1950, and by our own Prime Minister's slightly earlier visit to Persia.

Persia to-day is on the threshold of a new era of prosperity. She is eagerly seizing her opportunities and striving to conquer her geographical handicaps. Her population of 14 million people consists almost entirely of Muslims. Under the guidance of the late Shahenshah and his son (the present ruler) they have survived the shock of two World Wars and have embarked on a very great programme of social and industrial development, while at the same time preserving their Islamic religion and culture.

The discovery of oil has poured wealth into Persia and opened up endless prospects of work and prosperity. With the help of America, prodigious sums are to be spent in the next seven years on agriculture and irrigation ($165 millions), exploration and opening of new oilfields ($35 millions), roads, railways, ports and airfields ($165 millions), mines and industries ($100 millions), drinking water and electricity for towns ($35 millions), hygiene and education ($100 millions). A dollar being worth about 4 rupees (Pakistan), this Seven Years' Plan compares well with our own great projects.

Much of the money, too, will be spent in the rural areas, for, as in the case of Pakistan, the great majority of the people of Persia are cultivators of the soil. As a writer recently remarked, 'both States are wedded to a policy of progressive revolution on modern scientific lines for building a welfare state on the principles of Islamic Socialism. It is little wonder, therefore, that both countries have forged friendly relations'.

It is unfortunate that in the first few years of Pakistan's existence the same close friendship has not prevailed between us and our other Islamic neighbour, Afghanistan. To Pakistanis this is a great disappointment, for at the beginning it was a comfort to think that immediately to our west lay a nation which shared with us a common religion, a common racial history, and a common cultural system. It therefore came as a shock to learn that Afghanistan was the only country to oppose Pakistan's admission to the United Nations Organization in 1948.

For a short while there were hopes of a better understanding through an exchange of Ambassadors. In 1949, however, the Afghan Government protested against a statement made by our Governor-General that the North-West Frontier Province formed an integral part of Pakistan. The Afghan rulers also supported a demand by a very small section of discontented tribesmen to form an independent country out of tribal and Pakistan territory under the name of 'Pashtoonistan'. The vast majority of our N.W. Frontier tribesmen much prefer to remain true Pakistanis, because they know this is in their best interests. We, for our part, have respected the international boundary, known as the Durand Line, which long existed during the days of British rule, and we have no desire to take one square inch of Afghan territory. Nor can we agree to surrender any of our own land. Nevertheless, some tribal outlaws, with the help of Afghan regular soldiers, attempted a raid on Pakistan territory in 1950. The invaders were immediately driven back into Afghanistan by our Armed Forces.

Unlike Turkey, Iraq, Persia, and Pakistan, Afghanistan has made little progress during the last half-century. It has remained a poor country, with its education backward and its industries undeveloped. The real spirit of Islamic democracy has not yet been awakened among its twelve million inhabitants, who have long been heavily taxed and kept in an unenlightened condition. Pakistan could do much to help the Afghan nation, even as we have already brought far greater prosperity and contentment to the tribal areas. The Afghans are a supremely brave and hardy people, with whom we have many ties of kinship.

Kashmir, whose ultimate fate has still to be decided, has been one of Pakistan's greatest problems. It was always included in the Muslims' plans for the creation of Pakistan. When the Mountbatten Award was made in 1947, partitioning India, to the surprise of all people Kashmir was not included in either of the newly founded countries of Pakistan and Bharat. The choice was apparently left to the Hindu Maharaja, who ruled as a complete autocrat over the State. Kashmir is as big a territory as Western Punjab. Its total population was about four millions, of whom (including both Jammu and Kashmir State) 78 per cent. were Muslims. The Maharaja failed to realize that it was his duty to his subjects to join Pakistan. His troops began to drive away all the Muslims.

The tragedy that followed is well known. His subjects rose in rebellion, and the Maharaja in a panic declared his accession to Bharat. Disorder spread all over the land, and thousands of Muslim refugees lost their lives, while their villages were destroyed. Bharati troops were flown to Kashmir to prevent the Azad Kashmir Government from liberating the country. Pakistan had to send its own Armed Forces to protect the refugees who were still fleeing from Kashmir. Pakistan and Bharat stood on the verge of open war. After vain attempts to arrive at a settlement, the dispute was referred to the United Nations Organization, which sent its own mediators to suggest peaceful ways of solving this very serious problem.

Given peace and good government, Kashmir can become a happy and prosperous land once more. It possesses great forest and mineral wealth and the fertility of its soil is proverbial. Being one of the most beautiful countries in the world, it was for a long time a renowned tourist centre and an international playground for health-seekers and holiday-makers.

With Bharat itself the people of Pakistan are always seeking to establish a better understanding. Being historically associated, and geographically part of the same sub-continent, the two countries are mutually dependent on each other for many of the necessities of life. Roughly, thirty-five million Muslims still live in India and at least fifteen million Hindus have their homes in Pakistan. Although many grave problems remain to be solved between the two countries, with mutual toleration and wise statesmanship they can exist in peace side by side. They co-operate mutually in many different activities and carry on an extensive trade. It was a hopeful gesture of goodwill when Pakistan made a gift of 15,000 tons of grain to help the afflicted people of Assam after the great earthquake there in 1950.

Burma, our most easterly neighbour, is now an independent republic with a population of nearly fifteen millions, and covers an area of 262,000 square miles. Its capital is the seaport of Rangoon. Burma was conquered by the British nearly a hundred years ago and in 1886 was formed into a province of British India. In 1935 it became a separate British possession. During the 1939-45 World War it was invaded and occupied by the Japanese, who, however, were driven out in 1945 by the Western Allies. Many of our Pakistani soldiers fought with great valour in the Burma campaigns. When the war ended, Burma was given its complete independence, and decided to leave the British Commonwealth.

Our relations with Burma are friendly and a good deal of trade is carried on between our two countries. Burma is one of the most important rice-growing regions and also possesses immense forests of valuable timber like teak. Its oilfields are not far from our own Chittagong Hill Tracts and are among the greatest in the world. There are also rich lead, tin, silver, and ruby mines. Cotton, rubber, tobacco, and groundnuts are extensively grown. The people are mainly Buddhists, but many Muslims, Hindus, Mongolians, and Malayans have also made their homes in Burma and have done much to develop her agriculture, industries, and commerce.

Two other powerful countries lie just beyond our immediate neighbours and are of special importance to Pakistan. Only Kashmir State and a thin strip of

Afghanistan separate us from Soviet Russia, whose nearest States are Kazakhstan and Kirgizhstan, where many of the population are Muslims. Our Government opened an Embassy in Moscow in 1949 and the U.S.S.R. has sent an Ambassador to Karachi. The two countries are thus on a friendly footing with each other, although trade between the two is not yet extensive. While the Communist Government of Russia does not impart much information about developments in its Asiatic territories, it is reported that many industrial cities have begun to grow up there north of Afghanistan and Kashmir.

With the spread of Communism in China, Pakistan comes into direct contact with powerful Far Eastern neighbours. For a short distance, in fact, we have a common frontier with Sinkiang, where there is a Central People's Government to which Pakistan has given recognition. A Pakistani Consulate-General has been established at Kashghar. Some of the people there are Muslims.

Eastern Pakistan is separated from the main Chinese central plain only by Burma. Owing to the heavily forested mountains in this region, there is at present very little direct contact with the central portions of China, but trade proceeds via Burma and also by the long sea route via Penang. Arrangements are being made to bring about an exchange of Ambassadors with the Central People's Government at Nanking.

Although Communistic theories do not harmonize with the ideals of Islamic democracy, it is of importance to Pakistan that she should be able to understand the position in the Communist countries, especially as there is nothing in Asia that does not in some way affect our own country. China, with its 454 millions of inhabitants and its enormous natural resources, has a vital influence on world peace. For forty years it has suffered turmoil through invasion and civil war; but the history of its people shows that it is not a country which any others can ignore. The war which has raged in Korea since June 1950 has brought China into unique prominence.

CHAPTER XXV

THE UNITED NATIONS ORGANIZATION

The first thought of any nation which wishes to travel along the road of Progress is to make sure of remaining at peace with its neighbours. This is particularly true in the case of a young or small nation. History has repeatedly shown how easy it is for weaker countries to be drawn into war against their will and to suffer invasion and conquest. War is a destroyer of happiness and prosperity, a thing to be dreaded and shunned by weak or strong alike. It creates nothing but death and misery, even to the victors—especially in modern warfare, because of the way in which civilian populations suffer. Long-range guns, explosive or fire-bombs, jet-propelled missiles, and atom bombs are fearful instruments, causing havoc far behind the actual battle-fronts.

Unfortunately, war has for thousands of years been the chief curse of the human race. In the olden days, when men lived in big tribes, it was perhaps more natural that they should look upon strangers with suspicion and take up their weapons to fight without the least attempt to parley. When the tribes grew into nations the same instinct was carried on. If enmity arose, or some ambitious leader wanted to make himself appear greater than others, the stronger would attack its weaker neighbours and rule over them or reduce them to slavery. Even in later times, when mankind became highly civilized, wars were a constant trouble to all countries. And this has continued until our own day.

All of us who read this book are old enough to remember that we have only recently seen the end of a second World War, in which twenty-nine countries fought together against eight others for roughly six years. A similar World War took place only twenty-five years earlier (1914–18), when over fifteen Allied nations fought against five on the other side. In both World Wars battles were fought in many different countries, millions of soldiers and civilians were killed or wounded, and great waste took place. Both these wars were started by Germany, which had carefully planned to make itself the ruler over all others. In 1914 it was the German Emperor who led his people to believe that they could conquer the world; in 1939 it was Hitler, whose example was followed by the leaders of Italy and Japan.

Although the Allies won the 1914–18 War, they did not form sufficient safeguards when peace returned. It is true that they set up a League of Nations, with headquarters at Geneva (in Switzerland), and that Germany, on becoming a member of the League, undertook not to go to war again. Many treaties were also made. Two big mistakes, however, undid all the good. In the first place, the League of Nations had no armed force with which to compel obedience from any country which dared to defy it. Secondly, so busy were the Allies with their own affairs that they failed to prevent Germany from rearming and growing too strong again.

Hitler at first built up his armies and made their weapons secretly. Then he openly defied the League by re-entering the Saar Valley (rich in coal and covered with factories) which had been taken away from Germany. He next marched his army without warning into Austria and proclaimed it to be united to Germany. A few

THE UNITED NATIONS ORGANIZATION

months later, in 1938, he invaded the prosperous country of Czechoslovakia, and seized it without a battle. The League of Nations could no nothing to prevent this, because it had no army of its own, and no single country felt strong enough to fight alone against the Germans. Even before these events, the Italians under Mussolini in 1935 had attacked and occupied Abyssinia, which they wished to make into a colony, while the world looked on helplessly.

Encouraged by his early successes in Austria and Czechoslovakia, Hitler in 1939 suddenly invaded Poland. The Poles, however, possessed an army and fought to defend their country. They had made an alliance with Great Britain, who had promised to help the Poles if the latter were attacked. Britain kept her promise, and, when the Germans refused to leave Poland alone, Britain declared war on Germany and her allies. France, being Britain's ally, joined in the struggle. Later Italy and Japan threw in their lot with Germany, while Russia, the United States, and several other countries entered the war on the side of the Western Allies.

Although at last the peace-loving countries, which had not prepared for war, were forced into the struggle, they were too late to prevent the great conflict. The League of Nations also had proved completely helpless. Germany, Italy, and Japan had gained such a long start by their secret preparations that at first they won many victories. Almost the whole of Western Europe was seized by Germany. Japan conquered a large part of Southeast Asia, including Indo-China, Malaya, the Dutch East Indies, Burma, most of China, and many Pacific islands; India and Australia were seriously threatened.

It took five years for the Western Allies to build up their strength. Huge armies, navies, and air-fleets had to be raised, trained, and properly equipped. Tens of thousands of factories in Britain, America, Canada, and Australia stopped making peace-time goods and poured out immense quantities of ammunition, guns, tanks, aeroplanes, and battleships. By degrees these were transhipped to the war zones. The Italians were driven out of Abyssinia; the Germans and Italians were completely beaten in North Africa; Italy was invaded and set free. Russia began to push back the huge German armies which had advanced far into Soviet territory; the Western Allied forces landed in France and chased Hitler's troops back into Germany. Poland was set free by the Russians; Belgium, Holland, and Denmark by the British and Americans. At last Berlin, the German capital, was taken, and there Hitler met his death. The war in the West thus came to an end. Japan was defeated in the Philippine Islands, Borneo, and Burma, and two atom bombs on Hiroshima and Nagasaki completely ended the Japanese will to fight any longer.

The end of the 1939-45 World War unhappily has not yet restored complete peace to the world. While the Nazi and Fascist dictators of Germany and Italy were destroyed and Japan's military party overthrown, the seeds of possible new conflicts were being sown. The greatest danger since then has been the determination of the Communists in Russia to spread their beliefs into the democratic countries and to replace the parliamentary system of government with 'Peoples' Republics' ruled by dictators. This would mean the end of the freedom of choice, and every individual would become the tool and the servant of 'the State', which would own everything, plan every detail of their existence, and manage even their private lives.

THE UNITED NATIONS ORGANIZATION

Not satisfied with sending their secret agents everywhere, the Communists have built up huge armies and air-fleets in Russia, where giant factories are making weapons and ammunition. The outside world is not allowed to know what is happening in Russia. The danger to peace was clearly seen when one of Russia's Communist allies, Northern Korea, defied the United Nations by suddenly invading Southern Korea in 1950, although the whole Korean country (which previously belonged to Japan) had been divided into two portions by the United Nations Organization. This time, however, peace-loving democracies were in a position to resist aggression, for they had agreed to lend their armed forces to UNO, so as to enable the latter to enforce obedience to the will of the world. Troops and planes were sent to help the South Koreans and many nations took part in this work.

This combined resistance to an aggresor was due to an important declaration—first made in 1942 by nineteen nations—that each would 'employ its full resources, military and economic', against the countries with which they were then at war. In 1943 the United States, Great Britain, the U.S.S.R., and China pledged themselves to form a general international organization to maintain world peace and security. In 1945 the Charter of the United Nations was signed by the representatives of fifty countries and UNO was thus founded. Since then, nine others have joined, including Pakistan.

The Appendix at the end of this book contains the full text of the Preamble and of Chapter I of this great Charter. A study of this will reveal that the United Nations have joined together to show their faith in the four fundamental human rights—'freedom of speech, freedom of religion, freedom from want, and freedom from fear'—as first stated by the late President Roosevelt. The members of UNO are pledged to keep the world peaceful and by their joint efforts to prevent and remove any threats to peace. They have promised to bring about a settlement of all international disputes by peaceful means instead of by war; to develop friendship among nations; and to help in solving all international problems. Within UNO all members are absolutely equal: all have one vote each, so that the bigger and stronger nations have no advantage over the smaller ones. All agree not to use threats and not to attack others, though they keep the right to fight against an aggressor. They promise to help UNO to enforce its decisions and they agree also not to help any State which has offended UNO. There will be no interference, however, in matters that concern the purely internal affairs of any State.

In order to carry on its business, UNO has a General Assembly consisting of all its members; a Security Council; an Economic and Social Council; a Trustee Council; an International Court of Justice, and a Secretariat. The Assembly may discuss any matters of international interest and make recommendations to promote world peace, encourage co-operation, and help all mankind. Every member-nation has one vote. A two-thirds majority of the members present and voting must be in favour for a decision to be reached on important questions. The General Assembly receives and considers annual and special reports from the Security Council and other United Nations organizations.

Of these the Security Council is the most important, for upon it falls the responsibility for preserving world peace and security. When dangerous disputes arise between any two countries, the Security Council holds an inquiry into the causes and calls upon the parties to settle their quarrel peacefully. If, in spite of this, either of the countries concerned continues to threaten, or actually attacks, the other, the Security Council is able to take forceful action against the aggressor. All members of the United Nations undertake to make available to the Security Council their armed forces and other forms of help, so that the offender can be compelled to obey. In other words, under the Charter, the United Nations Organization carries on war until the offender surrenders. This is very different from war between only the two countries originally involved in a dispute, because now the aggressor is made to understand that all are combined against an evil-doer.

Another way in which UNO benefits all mankind is through its Economic and Social Council, which promotes higher standards of living, full employment, and conditions of economic and social progress and development; also the solution of social, health, cultural, and educational problems, as well as universal respect for and observance of human rights and the 'four freedoms'. All member-countries pledge themselves to take joint and separate action in co-operation with UNO to achieve these purposes. The Economic and Social Council has set up nine general 'commissions', each to look after one field of work.

Pakistan has joined almost all these special bodies. Our country is, for example, a member of the International Labour Organization, which seeks to create lasting peace by improving the conditions in which men and women work and by raising their standard of living. This has led to the making of better factory laws, more reasonable hours of work, better housing for the working classes, 'Safety First' measures, and compensation for injuries. Through another special Commission, the Food and Agricultural Organization, UNO tries to raise the levels of food and the standards of living of all people; to help land workers to produce more and better crops, and to arrange a fair share of food for all the nations.

Of importance to Pakistan also is the work of UNESCO (United Nations Educational, Scientific, and Cultural Organization), whose purpose is to spread education and knowledge among all people. Pakistan has been able to take part in several important world conferences on education, arranged by UNESCO, and has received much valuable information and guidance. One act of generosity which has been very helpful took the form of a gift of $15,000 worth of radio sets from UNESCO for distribution among our educational organizations and institutions. UNESCO is making Pakistan better known to other nations.

Another United Nations special commission in which Pakistan is greatly interested is the WHO (World Health Organization). This body aims at the highest possible health level for all nations. Its experts and research workers visit all countries to help in the study of diseases and in the discovery of remedies. Through WHO splendid research laboratories are established, and all other ways of preventing epidemics are given every possible assistance. WHO has given several special scholarships to our Pakistani doctors to enable them to carry on higher studies abroad. It was WHO that sent us a 'Malaria Control Demonstration Team', which has done very successful work in Mymensingh District, and which has been

THE UNITED NATIONS ORGANIZATION 215

training our Pakistani doctors and health workers in special methods of putting an end to malaria.

We owe much gratitude also to UNICEF (United Nations International Children's Emergency Fund) for helping to plan and carry out a great scheme to promote the health of Pakistan's children and their mothers. This has meant the growth of training schools for nurses and midwives and considerable improvements in women's and children's hospitals, as well as Maternity and Child Welfare Centres. UNICEF also did great work in feeding numbers of school-children at Karachi and in providing daily extra milk for refugee children in Pakistan. We are glad to think that our own country recently made a gift of wheat worth Rs.100,000 to UNICEF for refugees in Palestine, where both Arab and Jewish children were suffering hunger and distress.

One of the earliest commissions Pakistan joined on entering the United Nations Organization was ICAO (the International Civil Aviation Organization). This body studies all the problems of air travel and communications, and aims at the establishment of a world-wide standard of Civil Aviation safety and efficiency. Pakistan is also a member of UPU (Universal Postal Union), by which we are able to send our letters, parcels, and postal orders to all other parts of the world at rates accepted by all.

The trade of our country is further promoted by Pakistan having become a member of the World Bank and the International Monetary Fund. We belong also to the UNO group known as ECAFE (Economic Commission for Asia and the Far East), which for the first time in the world's history enables joint discussions to take place in Asia on the problems affecting all the countries there east of Persia, and including Australia and New Zealand. Agriculture, industries, technical training, trade, flood control, and research—all are included in ECAFE's field of study and of concerted action.

Already the United Nations Organization has proved its value in many directions. It put an end to warfare between Arabs and Jews in Palestine. It planned the basis of a settlement of the post-war trouble in Indonesia. It arranged the withdrawal of British and French troops from Syria and Lebanon, and of Russian troops from Iran. It outlawed group wars. It challenged aggression in Korea. It has steadily been making a better world for all people. For these reasons Pakistan has given UNO its ready and loyal support—and, by so doing, Pakistan is making its contribution to freedom, justice, toleration, and world brotherhood and peace.

CHAPTER XXVI

THE MAKERS OF PAKISTAN

EVERY nation takes pride in remembering its great men and women. To their heroic actions or inspired wisdom the people owe the greatness of their present position in the world. Some may have been brave kings or leaders of armies, like the Emperor Akbar or the Duke of Marlborough. Others were poets, thinkers, and artists, such as Shakespeare, Goethe, Leonardo da Vinci, or Sa'adi Shirazi. Many were doers of noble deeds for the public welfare—Florence Nightingale, the first to create a proper nursing service; Grace Darling, the rescuer of shipwrecked sailors. Famous scientists, inventors, explorers, teachers, and doctors have, by their self-sacrificing example, become household names in many countries. Some perhaps have been well known only in their own countries; others, like Christopher Columbus or Charles Darwin, are remembered in world history.

So, too, in Pakistan we turn with gratitude and affection to all those persons who have shared in any way in the task of creating our country and leading it to freedom. Some of them lived long ago, before even the word 'Pakistan' was first spoken. A few took part in the actual making of our nation, but have to our great sorrow left the earthly scene. Many, we rejoice to think, are still with us and still working with high skill and intelligence to keep us on the road to progress and contentment. Pakistan has by no means been lacking in heroic figures and wise leadership.

Dearest to the hearts of all of us must ever be the actual founder of our country, the late Mohammed Ali Jinnah, to whom in our gratitude we gave the name of 'Quaid-i-Azam'. Without his leadership the Muslims of the Indian sub-continent would have had immense difficulty in finding a way to save Islam from the threat of Hindu supremacy. Without his superhuman efforts in the first two years there might have been vast mistakes and weaknesses in the process of setting up our new State. Although by then frail and old, he worked with a vigour that put young persons to shame. The strain of his last two years proved too great for a man of his age, and his health broke down. Mohammed Ali Jinnah died for his country as truly as could any warrior on the field of battle. He was the first and ever will be the greatest of Pakistanis.

Born in Karachi in 1876 of a wealthy merchant family, Mohammed Ali Jinnah went to England at the age of 16, and became a barrister of Lincoln's Inn. On returning to India he practised at Karachi and later at the Bombay Bar. In 1909 he began his long political career, being elected from the Bombay Presidency Muslim constituency to the newly created Indian Legislative Council, where he became a renowned debater. At an early date he became a member of the Indian National Congress, which was the only All-India political organization then aiming at self-government by rightful means. When, however, a new school of thought arose in Congress under leaders like Tilak, Bepin Chandra Pal, and Khaparde, who not only preached violence, but also gave a 'Hindu-revival' touch to the struggle, Mr. Jinnah became alarmed and devoted himself to the cause of the Muslim League, which had just been founded.

For the next few years the Muslim League worked side by side with the Congress, and in 1916 the Lucknow Pact (framed chiefly by Mr. Jinnah) was signed by both these bodies. The main point of agreement between them was that the Muslims should be given separate electorates and a fixed proportion of seats in the Legislative Council. When in 1919 limited self-government was granted to India, the Congress refused to work the reforms, and Mr. Gandhi opened his Non-violent Non-co-operation campaign. Mr. Jinnah strongly opposed this new idea and resigned from the Congress.

Now devoting himself to the affairs of the Muslim League, Mr. Jinnah in 1929 summed up the Muslim demand in his famous 'Fourteen Points', and at the Round Table Conferences in London insisted that they should be granted. He won a great victory when, because the Hindus and Muslims could not agree among themselves, the British Prime Minister gave an Award, which allowed nearly all the Muslim claims. The League accepted the Award, which the Congress bitterly attacked. Under Mr. Jinnah's guidance, also, the Muslim League agreed to work the 1935 Reforms.

By this time Mr. Jinnah had become convinced that the Hindus were aiming at establishing their own domination over the whole sub-continent of India. He reunited all the Muslim groups and made the Muslim League their rallying-point. When in 1936 his offer of coalition ministries was refused by the Congress, and Pandit Jawaharlal Nehru incorrectly claimed that there were only two parties in the country (the British Government and Congress), Mr. Jinnah retorted that there was also a third party—the Muslim nation. By 1940 Mr. Jinnah felt that there could be no hope of justice and impartiality under Hindu majorities, and he declared in favour of the establishment of Pakistan as an independent sovereign State, 'where Muslims would be in a majority, and where they could pursue their own way of life and develop according to their own genius'.

When his dream came true at last in 1947, the Quaid-i-Azam took over the reins of the young State as its first Governor-General. For the next thirteen months he laboured unceasingly for his country. There were tremendous problems to be solved, thousands of arrangements to be made so that good government should be ensured, while the strained relations with Bharat were a constant anxiety. Sleeping only four hours a day, Mr. Jinnah found time to give his attention to everything. He was present at all important ceremonies and gatherings. He made a complete tour of the country. He supervised the planning of the whole life of the nation. His steadying influence calmed the fiercest excitement. As the 'Father of the Nation' he could persuade, drive, and advise as no one else could. It was all too much for his frail body. In September 1948 his heart suddenly failed. 'He had worked himself to death, but had contributed more than any other man to Pakistan's survival,' wrote an English onlooker. On Faith, Unity, and Discipline he built; on these three foundations Pakistan will enduringly continue.

While Mohammed Ali Jinnah was the actual architect of Pakistan, other notable thinkers and men of action have played a part in the course of events which led to the creation of the new State. In some cases their influence may appear indirect; nevertheless, they shared in the final result because they gave a new turn to the thoughts and desires of earlier generations, even though they did not perhaps dream of the real shape of the things to come.

Such a personage was Hazrat Sayed Jamaluddin Afghani, one of the inspirers of modern Islamic revival. His connexion with Pakistan is perhaps not obvious at first glance, but when the width and depth of his influence are understood, one realizes that the spirit which shone through his mind has survived to our day. Born in the village of Saedabad (or Asadabad) near Hamadan, in the Kunnar valley of Afghanistan, in 1839, Jamaluddin was a 'boy prodigy'. He gathered a mass of learning which astonished Kabul, where his father (Sayed Safdar) was a scholar courtier. At the age of 18, having acquired all the knowledge that Afghanistan could give, Jamaluddin set out on a unique career of travel and teaching which took him to over fifteen different countries and filled forty years of his life.

That was an age when Islam had not yet fully recovered from the blows it had suffered between the fall of Seringapatam in 1799 and the naval disaster of Navarino in 1827. Turkey had become 'the sick man of Europe', and the influence of the West was still feared. A Muslim revival had nevertheless begun, and Jamaluddin threw himself heart and soul into the task of warning the Islamic countries to unite. Wherever he went he founded newspapers to spread this message of Pan-Islamism and preached the twofold policy of a great defensive alliance of the whole Muslim world to preserve itself from destruction, and, secondly, a study of the technique of Western progress so as to learn the secrets of European power. His self-imposed mission took him four times to India (where he was imprisoned), Egypt, Persia, Turkey, Russia, Germany, Iraq, Syria, America, England, France, Arabia,

Afghanistan. He learnt to speak and write fluently in seven widely different languages.

This political crusade had a particularly deep effect in Egypt, where great leaders like Zaghlul Pasha came under his spell and opened the campaign of 'Egypt for the Egyptians', which, after half a century of effort, brought complete independence to that land. Abdul Hamid, who had become Sultan of Turkey, and Caliph, recognized Jamaluddin's value and made him chief of his Pan-Islamic propaganda. The strain of so active a life broke his health, and in 1897 he died in Constantinople at the age of 60.

Among the countries in which Jamaluddin's teachings bore fruit was India. Here he produced a deep impression on thinkers like Sir Syed Ahmed Khan, Dr. Mohammed Iqbal, Moulvie Cheragh Ali, Syed Amir Ali, and S. Khuda Bukhsh. It was this influence that gave courage to our early Muslim Liberals to proceed with their advocacy of Islamic unity and Islamic progress. Out of these efforts came the set of circumstances which made our people realize that the Muslims were a separate nation from the Hindus, and led to the ultimate creation of the new Islamic State of Pakistan. Without the inspiration of Jamaluddin's Pan-Islamic unity, events might not have taken the same course. He thus played a vital part in the founding of our nation.

One of the first to see that the Muslims had fallen behind other communities in general prosperity and advancement in the India of the second half of the last century was Sir Syed Ahmed Khan (1817–99). He knew that this was due to the after-effects of the 'Indian Mutiny' of 1857 and the suppression of Muslims, together with the final collapse of the Moghal Empire.

Confiscations of Muslim property and the replacement of Muslim ruling chiefs by Hindus reduced many to poverty. The court and official language was changed from Persian to English. The Hindus quickly saw their chance, and showed great eagerness to co-operate with the English, who were their new masters. As the schools no longer taught Persian and Arabic, the Hindus took to learning English, and in this way became better qualified for Government service. With all this the Muslims would have nothing to do and their condition grew worse.

It was at this stage that Syed Ahmed Khan began to urge the Muslims not to be left behind, but to take to modern education. They began to realize also that he was striving to show the British that they should allow the people to take a part in the government of their own country and grant them district boards and municipalities as well as admission into the Legislative Councils. Alarmed by Hindu attempts to abolish Urdu, he was one of the earliest to foresee the danger of Hindu domination in the political sphere. He found, however, that his Muslim friends often objected to sending their sons to Government colleges, because there was no provision there for Islamic education. Syed Ahmed then made his great contribution to the Muslim cause; he set up at Aligarh a residential college, where both Arabic and religious knowledge were compulsory, and where English and Western subjects were taught. He proved to the satisfaction of all Muslims that there was no Quranic obstacle to the attainment of modern knowledge.

Aligarh was later raised to the status of a university, and it enabled Muslims to enter public life and hold important positions, as well as to become leaders of our own people. Many of our most notable Pakistanis of to-day graduated at Aligarh—among them being our present Governor-General (Khwaja Nazimuddin), the Prime Minister (Mr. Liaquat Ali Khan), the Finance Minister (Mr. Ghulam Mohammed), and Maulana Mohammed Ali, the Khilafat leader. As in their case, Aligarh became to all a symbol of the Muslims' desire for social progress as well as for Islamic unity. Both these ideas played a great part in Sir Syed Ahmed's life, for he believed that 'the Muslims were a nation who could not and must not be submerged in a system of government by majority vote' (Richard Symonds, in *The Making of Pakistan*).

Yet another thinker who did much to correct the idea that Islam was opposed to progress was Syed Amir Ali (1849-1928), the first Indian Muslim to become a High Court Judge and the first Indian to attain the rank of a British Privy Councillor. He published several scholarly works, such as *The Spirit of Islam* and *History of the Saracens,* in which he boldly urged reforms to modernize Islam in general. Although he did not take a very active part in politics, he led a deputation to the Secretary of State for India (Lord Morley) in 1909, and persuaded him to give Muslims separate electorates in the Minto-Morley Reforms of that year. Syed Amir Ali's knowledge of Mohammedan Law was exceptionally deep, and lent authority to his views on social reform, modern education, and the betterment of the position of women. Although he did not directly contribute to the idea of a separate State of Pakistan, his writings helped to create an atmosphere favourable to the later acceptance of such a proposal.

Far more direct was the influence of Allama Mohammed Iqbal, the poet, who eagerly accepted the notion of Pakistan, and wrote with enthusiasm on that subject. A deep student of philosophy, he believed that life's justification lay in ceaseless action, based upon the Oneness of God and the unity of Islam. It was he who first conceived the idea of a separate Muslim State in the Indian sub-continent—'a State in which', to quote our Minister for Industries, 'the genius of Islam would find its modern expression and would bring forth a new way of life, of freedom, and of hope, to the millions of Muslims, who for centuries had borne the burden of slavery: a State, in short, which would not be based on the accidents of birth, race, or colour, but on the people's adherence to a common ideology'.

Born in 1876 at Sialkot, Mohammed Iqbal became Professor of History and Philosophy at Lahore, when only 23 years of age. In 1905 he came to England and studied Philosophy at Cambridge. After taking his call to the Bar from Lincoln's Inn, he received the degree of Ph.D. at Munich. On his return to India, Iqbal soon made his influence felt among modern Islamic thinkers. He urged our people to understand the energy of Western civilization and to recreate within themselves the powers of self-realization which had once made their ancestors great. Poetry was the medium through which he found himself best able to spread this message.

In 1925 Iqbal turned to politics, and was elected to the Punjab Legislative Council. In 1930 he advocated the formation of a North-West Indian Moslem State. In that same year he published his great philosophical work, *The Reconstruction of Religious Thought in Islam,* based upon six lectures which he had delivered at Madras, Hyderabad, and Aligarh. This book was a deeply significant attempt to create a new philosophy of Islam, bringing in a wide study of modern scientific development as well as purely philosophical thought. It was just before his death, in 1938, that the idea of a separate Islamic State, named Pakistan, was brought to his notice, and met with his cordial approval. By his earlier poems and writings Iqbal had already done much to prepare the ground for its acceptance and fulfilment.

EPILOGUE

IT is right that we should thus honour the memory of those to whom we owe our nationhood, our ideals, and our independence. Alas, none of the five great men whose careers we have just recounted remains with us to-day. But Pakistan will with everlasting gratitude remember her founders. The sincerest homage we can pay to them is to live as they would have desired us to live—in faith, unity, and discipline. In our hearts we enshrine the last message that the Quaid-i-Azam imparted to our people: 'Nature has given you everything. You have got unlimited resources. The foundations of your State have been laid, and it is now for you to build, and build as quickly and as well as you can. So go ahead, and I wish you God speed! Pakistan Zindabad.'

APPENDIX

THE CHARTER OF THE UNITED NATIONS

Preamble

WE, the peoples of the United Nations, determined to save succeeding generations from the scourge of war, which twice in our lifetime has brought untold sorrow to mankind; and

to reaffirm faith in fundamental human rights, in the dignity and value of the human person, in the equal rights of men and women and of nations large and small; and

to establish conditions under which justice and respect for the obligations arising from treaties and other sources of international law can be maintained; and

to promote social progress and better standards of life in larger freedom;

and for these ends

to practise tolerance and live together in peace with one another as good neighbours; and

to unite our strength to maintain international peace and security; and

by the accepting of principles and the institution of methods to ensure that armed force shall not be used, save in the common interest; and

to employ international machinery for the promotion of economic and social advancement of all peoples, have resolved to combine our efforts to accomplish these aims.

Accordingly, our respective Governments, through representatives assembled in the City of San Francisco, who have exhibited their full powers found to be in good and due form, have agreed to the present charter of the United Nations, and do hereby establish an international organization to be known as the United Nations.

CHAPTER I

PURPOSES AND PRINCIPLES

Article 1

THE purposes of the United Nations are:

1. To maintain international peace and security, and to that end: to take effective collective measures for the prevention and removal of threats to the peace and for the suppression of acts of aggression or other breaches of the peace, and to bring about by peaceful means, and in conformity with the principles of justice and international law, adjustment or settlement of international disputes or situations which might lead to a breach of the peace;

2. To develop friendly relations among nations based on respect for the principle of equal rights and self-determination of peoples, and to take other appropriate measures to strengthen universal peace;

3. To achieve international co-operation in solving international problems of an economic, social, cultural, or humanitarian character, and in promoting and encouraging respect for human rights and for fundamental freedoms for all without distinction as to race, sex, language, or religion; and

4. To be a centre for harmonizing the actions of nations in the attainment of these common ends.

Article 2

The organization and its members, in pursuit of the purposes stated in Article 1, shall act in accordance with the following principles:

1. The organization is based on the principle of the sovereign equality of all its members.

2. All members, in order to ensure to all of them the rights and benefits resulting from membership, shall fulfil in good faith the obligations assumed by them in accordance with the present Charter.

3. All members shall settle their international disputes by peaceful means in such a manner that international peace and security, and justice, are not endangered.

4. All members shall refrain in their international relations from the threat or use of force against the territorial integrity or political independence of any State, or in any other manner inconsistent with the purposes of the United Nations.

5. All members shall give the United Nations every assistance in any action it takes in accordance with the present Charter, and shall refrain from giving assistance to any State against which the United Nations is taking preventive or enforcement action.

6. The organization shall ensure that States which are not members of the United Nations act in accordance with these principles so far as may be necessary for the maintenance of international peace and security.

7. Nothing contained in the present Charter shall authorize the United Nations to intervene in matters

which are essentially within the domestic jurisdiction of any State or shall require the members to submit such matters to settlement under the present Charter; but this principle shall not prejudice the application of enforcement measures under Chapter VII.

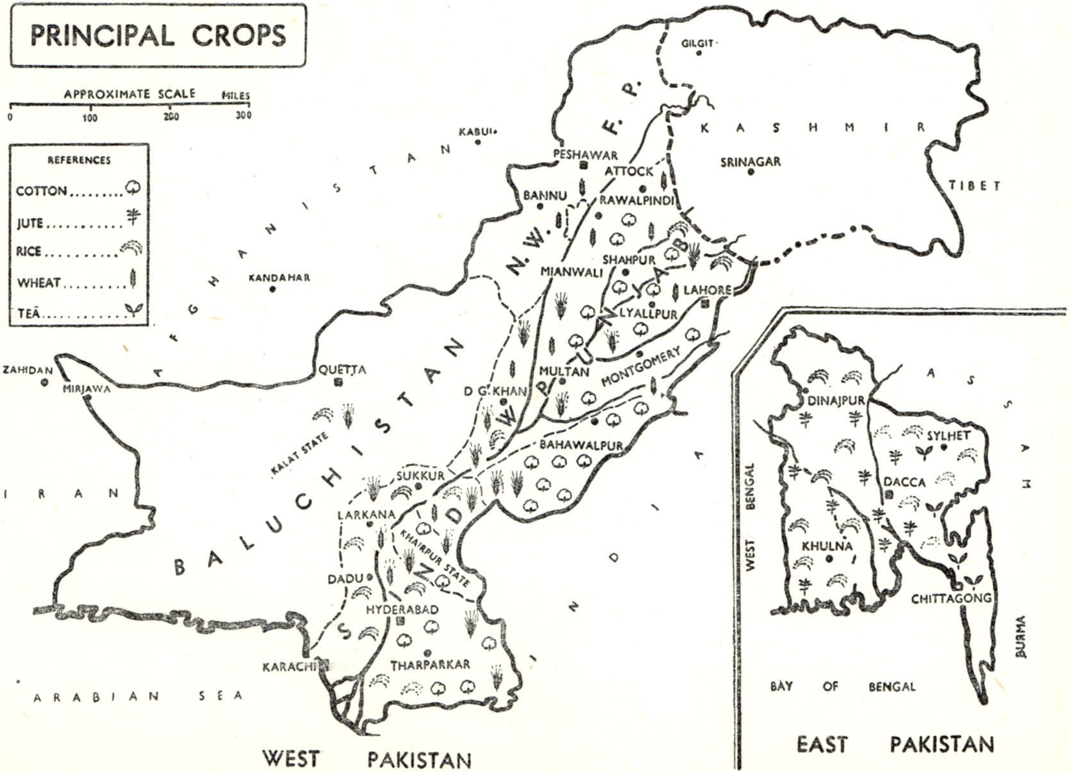
PRINCIPAL CROPS
APPROXIMATE SCALE
MILES
0
100
200
300
REFERENCES
COTTON
JUTE
RICE
WHEAT
TEA
WEST PAKISTAN
EAST PAKISTAN
KASHMIR
TIBET
GILGIT
SRINAGAR
N.W.F.P.
PESHAWAR
ATTOCK
RAWALPINDI
BANNU
MIANWALI
SHAHPUR
LAHORE
LYALLPUR
MONTGOMERY
MULTAN
BAHAWALPUR
PUNJAB
D G. KHAN
BALUCHISTAN
QUETTA
KALAT STATE
SIND
SUKKUR
KHAIRPUR STATE
LARKANA
DADU
HYDERABAD
THARPARKAR
KARACHI
ARABIAN SEA
AFGHANISTAN
KABUL
KANDAHAR
IRAN
ZAHIDAN
MIRJAWA
INDIA
ASSAM
BURMA
WEST BENGAL
DINAJPUR
SYLHET
DACCA
KHULNA
CHITTAGONG
BAY OF BENGAL

PRINTED IN GREAT BRITAIN BY
HAZELL WATSON AND VINEY LTD
AYLESBURY AND LONDON

ATLANTIC OCEAN
ENGLAND
EUROPE
BERLIN
VIENNA
LENINGRAD
UNION OF SOVIET SO
ISTANBUL
BLACK SEA
KAZAK
TURKEY
CAIRO
IRAQ
IRAN
AFGHANISTAN
KASH-MIR
WEST PAKISTAN
DELHI
ARABIA
MECCA
AFRICA
KARACHI
JUNAGADH (PAKISTAN)
IND
BOMBAY
HYDER-ABAD
ADEN
ARABIAN SEA
ENGLISH MILES
0 200 400 600 1000
COLOMBO
INDIAN OCE
60
70
0
20
40
60
50
40
30
20
10
0
40
50
60
70
80